THE

TGG

WAY

MATT GARRETT

THE
TGG
WAY

THE NUMBERS AREN'T THE
MOST IMPORTANT THING FOR A BUSINESS,
THEY ARE THE **ONLY THING**

Advantage®

Published by Advantage, Charleston, South Carolina.
Member of Advantage Media Group.

ADVANTAGE is a registered trademark, and the Advantage colophon is a trademark of Advantage Media Group, Inc.

Printed in the United States of America.

10 9 8 7 6 5 4 3 2 1

ISBN: 978-1-59932-519-4
LCCN: 2017946905

Book design by Megan Elger.

This publication is designed to provide accurate and authoritative information in regard to the subject matter covered. It is sold with the understanding that the publisher is not engaged in rendering legal, accounting, or other professional services. If legal advice or other expert assistance is required, the services of a competent professional person should be sought.

Advantage Media Group is proud to be a part of the Tree Neutral® program. Tree Neutral offsets the number of trees consumed in the production and printing of this book by taking proactive steps such as planting trees in direct proportion to the number of trees used to print books. To learn more about Tree Neutral, please visit **www.treeneutral.com.**

Advantage Media Group is a publisher of business, self-improvement, and professional development books. We help entrepreneurs, business leaders, and professionals share their Stories, Passion, and Knowledge to help others Learn & Grow. Do you have a manuscript or book idea that you would like us to consider for publishing? Please visit advantagefamily.com or call **1.866.775.1696.**

TABLE OF CONTENTS

A WORD FROM THE AUTHOR xi

INTRODUCTION 1
The Only True Accounting

CHAPTER 1 9
Why Own a Business?

CHAPTER 2 17
Staying on Track

CHAPTER 3 23
Accounting Has Stood the Test of Time

CHAPTER 4 27
The Three Rules of Accounting
(That Business Owners Must Know)

CHAPTER 5 53
The Triple Bottom Line

CHAPTER 6 . . . . **63**

Net Operating Income and
Your Business Model

CHAPTER 7 . . . . **85**

Cash from Operations and Net Equity

CHAPTER 8 . . . . **91**

Key Performance Indicators

CHAPTER 9 . . . . **105**

The Happiness Metric

CONCLUSION **109**

Where Do We Go from Here?

APPENDIX **113**

TGG's Twenty Beliefs about
Small Business Accounting

A WORD FROM THE AUTHOR

I am an entrepreneur/accountant/investor. I am an optimistic contrarian. I love breaking the status quo and trying new things. I rarely believe in rules, and I have a general disdain for authority. I am a libertarian thinker (not political in any way), and I love proving people wrong. So why did I write this book about accounting?

First, I struggle with problems every day where the answer is not black and white. I constantly make judgment calls, and sometimes the best answer is not to solve the problem but to wait for the problem to solve itself. This is the life of an entrepreneur.

Second, the only thing that makes my decisions easier is information. For the most part, the more information I have, the better decisions I make. The more I use the numbers, facts, and figures, the safer my business becomes.

Interestingly, accounting and entrepreneurism seem to require opposing skill sets, and yet they are incredibly symbiotic. Accounting requires a linear, right-versus-wrong mind-set. The system of accounting the world uses today has not fundamentally changed in over five hundred years. For centuries, merchants and entrepreneurs have faced the same pressures and turned to accounting for guidance.

This is a book about accounting principles for entrepreneurs, and these principles are not complicated. I know from experience, however, that most small businesses today do not know enough about accounting, and they pay the price for not paying close attention to the numbers. In the pages ahead, you will see clearly why, when it comes to profitably running a business, the numbers are not the *most important* thing—they are the *only* thing.

INTRODUCTION

The Only True Accounting

My current firm, TGG Accounting, is a byproduct of another pursuit that did not work out. Originally, my team and I were trying to found a boutique investment bank. The idea was that we were going to help small business owners negotiate sales of their companies.

Almost immediately, however, we ran into a problem. The firm's first five clients all had very poor accounting. It did not take long to realize that the accounting would need to be cleaned up before a business sale would be possible. I began hiring accountants to work on our clients' books. More and more businesses began coming to us to sell, and nearly all of them needed to clean up their books. About nine months into our endeavor, something startling happened. After we straightened out their books, the owners changed their minds about selling. They found that they were making more money than they realized. More importantly, they had peace of mind because they knew where they were financially and, equally important, they knew where they were going. Best of all, they had the confidence that business could be fun once they understood their financials and how to use them.

The investment banking business model lasted less than a year. There was a much more immediate need to help business owners with their accounting and with the internal management of their finances. For the next few years, my team worked with no more than a dozen clients, figuring out all the systems and processes and best practices to put in place. These accounting and finance best practice solutions slowly became what we know today as "The TGG Way."

The methodology of the TGG Way is based on time-tested accounting principles that have not changed in five hundred years. The benefits of implementing the TGG Way are:

- peace of mind,

- significant cost savings and higher profits,

- increased cash flow, and

- elevated business value for the owners.

Unfortunately, many businesses fail because they run out of cash. In most cases, this end is avoidable (if they saw it coming). Still, many businesses run out of cash because they do not understand accrual-based accounting—the *only* true accounting—which in its purest sense comes down to *recording transactions when they occur from a real economic standpoint.*

Take the example of Susan. Susan wanted to start a T-shirt business to take advantage of quirky trends and the availability of printing on demand. She began by designing shirts. Her work was very good, and she found high demand for her shirt designs. Very quickly, Susan had to turn her attention to producing those shirts. She engaged an on-demand textile screen printer and negotiated the price.

"Give us $50,000," the T-shirt manufacturer said, "and we will get started on turning your designs into shirts."

Susan took out a second mortgage on her home and she wrote the check. Did she lose any money at that point? If Susan had been using "cash-based" accounting, she would consider it a loss.

But, from the perspective of accrual-based accounting, that payment was *not* a loss. The truth of Susan's situation was that $50,000 was being applied to the production of her inventory. Inventory is an asset, with real, tangible resale value. Susan's payment to produce inventory is not an expense. She made an investment in her product. She was buying something that she was going to then sell to make *more* money.

The problem for many small business owners is that they incorrectly consider the purchase of inventory an expense rather than an investment. When incorrectly accounting for inventory, three bad outcomes are typical:

1. Decisions about how much inventory to buy are based on cash availability. Business owners may miss opportunities or lose out on good business deals.

2. Business owners may believe they are making money when they are actually losing money. Without a clear understanding of the exact amount being made on each product, it is impossible to accurately price the product.

3. Business owners may be making profits but misunderstand the time it takes to collect cash. In this situation, a business may be profitable and yet go out of business due to a lack of cash.

For Susan, to achieve a clear understanding of her pricing and achieve true profitability, the time the expense is recorded in the books must match the sale of those shirts.

Thirty days after her submitting her designs for production, the T-shirts arrived from the manufacturer. They looked great. They were edgy and funny, exactly as Susan had envisioned. Susan was proud and confident.

Unfortunately, per Susan's deal, she had to pay the manufacturer another $50,000 upon delivery of the shirts. This is a typical situation in the clothing industry. A standard deal with her manufacturer is half down and half upon delivery.

Susan was now out $100,000 in cash, but she had not sold a single shirt. She was still confident in her abilities, but at this point she was "all in." She had taken all the money available from her home equity loan and had even taken $25,000 from her mother.

So the business question is this: Did Susan just lose another $50,000? Has she lost all her money (and her mother's money)? No, she just made an additional investment in her business and paid for her inventory.

Susan's business moved forward another thirty days. She needed to sell T-shirts, as she was running out of cash. She made cold calls and went door-to-door. She was effective and made deals with retailers who loved her designs and wanted to sell her shirts. They were impressed. The shirts looked awesome and the retailers were optimistic.

The retail locations needed the shirts in their stores, and Susan immediately sent her shirts to their various locations, in a typical deal, for sale on "consignment." Under these terms, Susan still owned the T-shirts. Even though the T-shirts were physically located at the retail locations, the shirts were still technically Susan's, and the risky part of this situation is that, if the T-shirts did not sell, they could be sent back to Susan without pay. This is a scary situation for any clothing business, but it is typical. Susan was nervous but still confident.

At this point, Susan no longer had the physical T-shirts in her possession. Her "asset," the T-shirt inventory, was sitting in retail shops around the country; but had she earned any revenue yet? Had she sold any shirts? No, Susan could not recognize any revenue until the stores sold her T-shirts. Additionally, she still had the inventory asset (the T-shirts) and would own those T-shirts until they were sold.

Finally, even after the T-shirts were sold, Susan would not get the cash from the retailer for at least forty-five days.

As you can see, Susan had put out $100,000 but would probably not get any cash back from that $100,000 for 90–120 days. This is an unfortunate situation, but it is standard operating procedure for many businesses, and without proper planning this situation may lead to running out of cash and being out of business.

Another problem Susan faced was whether she was making any money. If she were looking at her situation on a cash basis, she would think she had lost a ton of money while producing the shirts and that she would begin making a ton of money a few months after the shirts sold. Granted, it was easy in the beginning stages of the business to see that she was waiting for her initial order to sell, but what if she had multiple orders and multiple designs all selling and being produced at the same time? That would be much too complicated to keep in her head.

Finally, using cash-basis accounting, Susan wouldn't know whether she was selling her T-shirts for the right price or even making a profit on each shirt. To understand her position accurately, Susan looked at it from the perspective of accrual-based accounting—she matched up the revenue from selling the T-shirt with the expenses of making the T-shirt. Knowing those figures, she easily determined her appropriate pricing, eventually negotiated better deals with suppliers and retailers, and, most importantly, had the peace of mind that comes from knowing where her cash was going, what cash would be needed, and exactly how much money she was making.

Guessing leads to mistakes, and mistakes in business lead to losing cash, not realizing profits, and ultimately not hitting goals. Being a great designer helped Susan sell T-shirts. Accurate, accrual-based accounting helped her make money, and ultimately, five years later, she sold her T-shirt business for $15 million.

A Focus on Small Business

The principles in this book apply to any business, although I choose to work with smaller ones. My clients range from start-ups to firms bringing in about $75 million in revenue.

Most of those businesses have a game plan. They know what they want to accomplish as a business, but their accounting is often not on par with their plans. Only one in twenty small companies produce accurate financial statements.

Business owners tend to have an unfailing optimism. They would like to believe that the statistics do not apply to them. They are counting on succeeding. But, in certain industries, the failure rate is as high as 78 percent. On average, after four years, 55 percent of start-ups are out of business. So, statistically speaking, most businesses fail.[1]

If you are a small business owner, the odds are against you, and it is optimism that will get you through—but it cannot be blind optimism. If you think the rules do not apply to you, then you are wrong. If you are doing what everyone else does, you will endure

---

1   Keith Speights, "Success rate: What percentage of businesses fail in their first year?" USA Today, accessed May 31, 2017, https://www.usatoday.com/story/money/business/small-business-central/2017/05/21/what-percentage-of-businesses-fail-in-their-first-year/101260716/.

the consequences like everyone else. On a national basis, per the Brookings Institute, the business failure rate is 10 percent a year.[2] Every year, one in ten businesses fail.

Accounting, done properly, is a powerful tool for making a lot of money. It is far more than something that must be done to file taxes each year. By understanding utilization, proper accounting of inventory, the sales cycle, and the leverage you can get from a bank loan, you can magnify your business's net income and value.

In this book, we will delve into the mechanics and mathematics behind these principles. We will look at the formulas that govern them. This is not some kind of complex calculus; it is basic math. There is a simple beauty in the numbers, and that's what accounting is all about.

Clear, sensible accounting gives you a map by which you can see where you are going. Many small businesses use a misleading map, which is worse than no map at all. You need the right kind of accounting to direct you on the proper path with unfailing precision. As a business owner, you need to understand these fundamentals.

But accounting is boring! I get this all the time, and I must agree: Sometimes accounting is a little dry. However, it can be very exciting when you realize what it can do for you. If you understand the principles of accounting and follow them, you will certainly find accounting profitable. My clients always say it's a lot more fun when they see how much more money they can make. Who wouldn't get excited about doubling profits? Pay attention to the numbers and you can make it happen. Ignore them and you will be courting disaster.

---

2   Ian Hathaway and Robert E. Litan, "Declining Business Dynamism in the United States: A Look at States and Metros," The Brookings Institution, *Economic Studies at Brookings*, May 2014.

CHAPTER 1

Why Own a Business?

As a business owner, I believe in a "hierarchy of needs" much like Maslow's that every business must satisfy. Here they are, in order of importance:

1. **Don't fail.** Base your operations on sound accounting metrics and accountability so that your business will not fail.

2. **Become profitable.** Build the ideal business model and execute to a comfortable level of profitability.

3. **Increase stability.** The next recession is coming. Only those businesses with enough financial stability will survive.

4. **Achieve your goals.** Clearly outline the direction you want to go in your life. How will that vision be embodied in your business, and how will your business support you in achieving your goals?

5. **Thrive, develop others, and give back.** What can you do to make a greater impact than you ever dreamed? How can you use the numbers to enable others to achieve their dreams (employees, partners, shareholders, vendors, etc.)?

All businesses need a purpose and a vision that is larger than an individual. But at the core, a business must also serve the personal goals and needs of the owner. It is a prudent and patient business owner who puts their business first and themselves last. It is a foolish business owner who puts the business first and their life last. The difference between putting yourself last and your life first is the difference between the tortoise and the hare. Back in the 1960s Goldman Sachs had a business mantra that ended up creating one of the most powerful financial institutions in the world. Their philosophy was "long-term greedy." I love that concept because it embodies a winning mentality. Another way to view this concept is in the Bible (Ecclesiastes): "The race is not for the swift but for those who can endure."

Here is what it means in small business. The winners are the ones who focus on the long-term vision and goals of the business, excluding short-term personal desires. Having the discipline to forego the new car, lake house, airplane, and other immediate gratification impulses in favor of the long-term vision and success of the business is the epitome of winning. Too often, the enemy of long-term business success is impulse spending and short-term lifestyle enhancement.

However, putting your life goals and dreams first helps guide all business decisions. Most of a business owner's net worth is trapped in his or her business. The only way to unlock that value is to sell the business. Without conservative and disciplined short-term management of personal spending, a business owner can quickly ruin the value of the overall business. For this reason, it is important to never lose sight of long-term, important life goals but equally mandatory to ignore the short-term pull of wanton desire for immediate gratification.

An entrepreneur's personal goals and needs must be reflected in and supported by the financial statements. It is important to track both business and personal goals to make sure that businesses (in the long run) are fulfilling them. Both personal and business goals are a priority when setting up an accounting system.

I recently worked with a couple who own climbing gyms for children around the country. Were they building this business for their retirement, I asked, or was this a pursuit that they purely enjoyed? Did they want to develop new stores, or were they looking to sell the business?

The couple told me that, frankly, it was high time they started enjoying life more—and maybe got out to do some climbing themselves. They wanted to build the business to the point where they could take a lot more time off for their own pursuits.

These are basic questions for every business owner: How would you like to set the business up? What is it that you want to do? How will that impact your life in a positive way? From there, you can start to build a business plan and an accounting system that will support it.

The plan to meet a business's hierarchy of needs starts with the personal needs of the owner, then builds in the business goals, and finally wraps it all up with the business's financial architecture. A business that is going to be sold in the next twenty-four months would be structured very differently than one based on low risk and intended to last for a lifetime.

Knowing Where You're Going

A lot of people, when they talk to financial planners or retirement planners, are surprised to find themselves chatting about goals and dreams. They expected to be talking about investments and where the market was heading, not where their life was heading. Likewise, people sometimes are surprised to hear, "So, where are you going with your business?"

The only way advisors can help people is by knowing their goals. We all want similar things, but each of us is unique. Some of us may want to retire in Fiji, while others love our work so much that we expect to keep doing it until we die. Neither is right or wrong, but we must make sure we have accounting and financial systems that support our goals. The numbers are critical, but they serve us; we do not serve them.

The magic is in how business owners adapt fundamental principles to their personal situations. It becomes much easier if they get the fundamentals right. Think of it this way: You do not have to train for a marathon. But if you *do* train every day, follow a strict diet and exercise regimen, sleep, and do what we all know is right for personal health, then running that marathon is going to be a lot easier. Most business owners jump into their business as if they will be running a marathon the next day. They ought to get themselves fit first.

If the numbers are wrong, if the fundamentals are awry, how will you reach your goals? The paradox is this: The numbers are the only things that matter because they support your goals, which are the only things that really matter. If you have bad information, you will make bad decisions, and you will not achieve those goals.

To make good decisions, you need to ask the big questions about your business: Why am I doing this? What is it all about? What do I want to accomplish? How do I want to be remembered?

People find many routes to get what they want out of life. As an entrepreneur, I believe in human potential. If people put their minds to a task and work at it, they will prosper. But I also know that proper accounting is a powerful tool for making the most of that human potential.

I believe in the pursuit of purpose. You can't do things just for the money, but you can't do things without money, either. A sense of purpose motivates you to get the details right so that you make the money needed to fulfill your purpose. That is the paradox and challenge.

Accounting is a support mechanism for goals and dreams. It is a tool that allows you to reach your dreams and know when you are hitting them. It allows you to measure your progress on the way to success. Most importantly, it provides peace of mind that you know where you are today and where you are going.

A Mission to Promote Success

Small business is the engine that drives this country. Most people work for small businesses, and millions lose their jobs as 10 percent of those businesses fail each year—and the loss of each job affects several other jobs. The toll that small business failure takes on this country and on families is enormous. Many business owners have a significant amount of their personal net worth tied up in the business.[3] They may have taken out a second mortgage, incurred loans from banks, not taken paychecks so their employees could get paid, and/or enlisted the support of families and friends.

Some people blame their industry, overregulation and high taxation, the market, the economy, poor salespeople, bad bankers, and other outside forces for the rate of small business failure. I choose not to take a position on those issues. It is clear from the data that small businesses have failed at roughly the same rate for the past

---

3   "U.S. Trust Study Finds Five Common Attributes of Business Owners," Bank of America Newsroom, posted June 23, 2015, http://newsroom.banko-famerica.com/press-releases/global-wealth-and-investment-management/us-trust-study-finds-five-common-attributes-b.

thirty years. The truth in the numbers is that small businesses fail because they do not see the failure coming. My mission is to help small businesses, one by one, to survive. Someone in your industry is successful, and that can and should be you.

I know how to start and run small businesses. I have done this for many years. I know what it takes to make a payroll. I know what it feels like to go without salary for a year so that you can sustain a business that you believe in. I understand the challenges and the stress.

The small business owners I work with are smart, dedicated, and hardworking. However, many of them didn't initially know how to manage the financial side of the business. Many of them got into it with a dream, a few dollars, and desire.

Take Bill, who says to himself, "Everybody says my chocolates are the best, so it is time I start a chocolate business!" Bill soon realizes that running a chocolate business has very little to do with making chocolate. He can sell his chocolates well, but soon his sales are outstripping his ability to make chocolates. Then he invests in a new plant, and he must figure out all the administration behind it: "Do I buy this baking equipment, or do I lease it? Do I buy a building, or do I rent? Do I get into long-term contracts with distributors, or do I have one contract with one wholesaler? *How do I do this?*"

These are the kinds of questions that the numbers can, in large part, help you answer. Using good financial statements will allow your business to succeed. They cannot *ensure* that you are successful; you must have the drive and desire for that. However, with excellent financial management, you can structure your business affairs so it is very hard to fail.

That is my mission in its simplest terms: to teach small business owners not only to avoid failing but also to thrive through excellent financial management.

CHAPTER 2

Staying on Track

All business owners have their own "why?" Some reasons are very clearly understood and easily articulated. Others are more intangible and lurk below the surface, woven into the entrepreneur's DNA.

Many business owners—like Susan, whom we met in the introduction—want the freedom that comes from owning one's own business. Susan has a strong urge to be independent. She doesn't want to rely on anyone for anything, particularly not her livelihood. Where others see risk and insecurity in owning and running their own business, Susan sees the opposite. By having her own business, she can control her own destiny. The risk of being downsized or laid off is nil.

Susan, like other independent-minded entrepreneurs, firmly believes in herself and her ability to provide her product or service better than anyone else. Her expertise and experience in her field cannot be matched. She knows what her customers want.

By building your business, you can make more money than you could working for someone else. You also give up the safety and security of a paycheck. With hard work and diligence, you can create wealth for your family, a legacy for your children and grandchildren.

This legacy will consist not only of the business's income and value but also of the example it set of the virtue of disciplined, focused effort.

Business has the power to move the world forward. Nothing can stop a coordinated effort toward a greater cause. Innovation, change, opportunity, and progress are all varieties of success. Perhaps your personal "why?" is a simple "I want to make a difference in the world."

What Can Derail Your Plan for Success?

Imagine this: You launch yourself whole hog into your business, the goal glowing in the distance. Your plans are well thought out and your enthusiasm unbridled. What could possibly go wrong? What could keep you from realizing your goals?

Well, you'll encounter plenty of obstacles, but most of them you can overcome. Let's look at some of them.

The primary obstacles are **business operational issues.** Business owners constantly encounter problems in the operation of their business, and managing those issues is their core responsibility. Many are energized by tackling big issues they can clearly see and understand: the shipment that arrives late or the machine that breaks down. They also relish the mysterious problem, the one they must wrestle with to understand and conquer: how to penetrate a new market or develop a game-changing, disruptive product. Most business owners can solve these types of problems. But even the best business owners will have difficulty dealing with issues they can't see.

Business owners can best prepare for these unexpected events by adequately addressing three key internal problems that can be roadblocks to achieving business goals. "Only three?" you wonder. By the time you've had your second cup of coffee, you've already had to deal with five problems that you felt could have been killers! Understood. But in my experience, these problems boil down to three fundamental issues that can be the death of a business.

#1: Lack of adequate cash flow is a problem that all business owners have faced, and it's a vexing one. Bill's chocolate business, from the last chapter, brings in money, but Bill always seems to be short of cash. He searches for the reasons. Are his collections too slow? Perhaps it's the off-season for the business, and he has not set aside sufficient reserves to weather this season. Despite the business's profits, there is never enough money.

Taxes, payroll, unexpected expenses, defaults by customers, or an ethically challenged employee can all divert cash from a business. As the cash flow slows to a trickle, the owner's frustration intensifies.

#2: Less than optimum profitability. Let's say an owner has a solid product and a sales force that could sell ice to Eskimos, but the business never seems to do much better than break even. How are the competitors charging less than our owner? Do they get volume discounts on their inventory? The business is profitable one quarter and then has a loss the following quarter—it yo-yos back and forth between profit and loss. This unpredictability makes it virtually impossible to get financing and creates an insecurity that permeates the business. Discouragement mounts, and the owner's dreams of financial independence and wealth creation seem out of reach.

#3: Not knowing where the business stands. If Bill doesn't know with certainty where his chocolate business stands and how it is doing at any given time, his decision making is impaired. He is anxious and uncertain and has no peace of mind about his decision to own his own business. Worst of all, his business could be on the path to failure and he wouldn't see it coming. Before he knew it, and without understanding why, his business would be dead.

Bill is perplexed. The business was profitable, but he's out of cash. He must pay taxes, even though the business is now unprofitable and out of money. The unexpected loss of a major customer requires him to cut 30 percent of his workforce to stay in business. His second-best customer then demands a 5 percent discount, and immediately his business is unprofitable. It may take a good deal of time for that to become apparent, however, and by that time it may be too late.

Sorry to be such a downer, but I wanted to focus your attention. I'm sure many of you have encountered at least one of these issues. I have experienced them all and have learned how to handle them: proper accounting.

By proper accounting, I mean accrual-based accounting done consistently with sound internal controls. Accrual-based accounting is black and white. It gives you a clear, sharply focused picture of how your business is doing at any given time. Proper accounting tells you where you have been, where you are, and where you are headed. It is like using a GPS for navigation instead of a compass and an intuitive, general sense of direction.

Unfortunately, many of the small businesses I have worked with are not even using a compass. They are proceeding through uncharted territory relying on just their instincts without any instrument telling them whether they're off course or not. Making the inevitable course correction without knowing the correct course is often unnerving and may cause more harm than good. In sailing, if a sailor is 3 percent off course, she is fifty yards off course after a mile, over a mile off course after fifty miles, and she might as well be in a different ocean after five hundred miles.

Proper accounting and the discipline that it brings to business processes can restore a sense of direction and provide confidence in the chosen course.

CHAPTER 3

Accounting Has Stood the Test of Time

Business owners have always needed to keep track of their income and expenses. The ancient Sumerians kept track of their business transactions on clay tablets, and as economies have become more complex and interdependent, business owners have needed improved tools to get a look at how their business was doing at any given time or how profitable different products and services were.

In the eleventh century, trade began to increase, stimulated by the Crusades and improvements in transportation. The Northern Italian city-states, Florence and Venice, excelled at trade and finance, and the merchants and their bankers needed a way to keep track of their far-flung ventures. Double-entry accounting developed to meet this need.

The oldest record of the use of double-entry accounting was found in a ledger kept by a Florentine merchant at the end of the thirteenth century. But it was Venetian businessmen who refined the methodologies and practices associated with double-entry accounting, and thus double-entry accounting came to be known as the Venetian Way.

By 1458, the first mention of double-entry accounting was included in a treatise on trading written by Benedetto Cotrugli. That book was not published, however, until 1593. In the interim, the acclaimed monk and mathematician Luca Pacioli described double-entry accounting in a treatise titled "Everything About Arithmetic, Geometry and Proportion," published in 1494. Bookkeeping was only one of five mathematical topics covered. The chapters on accounting were added to provide "complete instructions in the conduct of business" and "give the trader without delay information as to his assets and liabilities."[4]

Based on this work, Pacioli is often referred to as the "father of accounting." Pacioli, however, did not make such a claim. In fact, double-entry bookkeeping had been in use roughly two hundred years before Pacioli described it in his treatise.

The Venetian Way—double-entry accounting—has stood the test of time. While there have been some changes over the centuries, the basic principles developed by the Northern Italian mercantile community continue to be used today, from the corner grocery to General Electric, from Facebook to In-N-Out Burger. Double-entry accounting continues to be used almost eight hundred years after its introduction into commerce because the methodology produces accurate and dependable results. The numbers are true and trustworthy, which gives business owners comfort concerning the performance of their business.

Remember fourth-grade math? The teacher would give Sally an arithmetic problem and then have her check it by doing the problem in reverse and getting to the starting point.

---

4   "Life of Luca Pacioli," International Accounting Day website, accountants-day.info, accessed May 19, 2017, http://accountants-day.info/index.php/international-accounting-day-previous/77-luca-pacioli.

"Thank you, Sally," the teacher would say after Sally finished the problem with lightning speed. "I know that you are smart, and I know that you got the correct answer. But it is not always going to be this easy for you. Now, do it in reverse, show me your work, and prove to me that you really understand the concept."

A similar principle is at work in double-entry accounting. For every transaction, there are offsetting entries in the ledger. "Credits," appearing on the right-hand side of the ledger page are offset by "debits," appearing on the left-hand side. To check your work, you add the numbers on each side of the ledger. If the sum on the left-hand side of the page equals the sum on the right-hand side, the ledger is in balance and you know that the figures are correct.

A word of caution: Don't let the terms "debit" and "credit" mislead you by giving them a qualitative interpretation. Viewing these words in their contemporary context, you might think that a "credit" is good or positive while a "debit" is bad or negative. After all, if you are extended credit from a financial standpoint or given credit for some good work, that is generally viewed as positive. By contrast, "debit" means to reduce or take away—think debit card.

In fact, however, these terms have no qualitative connotations when used in accounting. In the language of accounting, they mean only right (credit) and left (debit). Their consistent usage since the advent of double-entry accounting attests to the continuing vitality and utility of this accounting system. The methodology and language of double-entry accounting has survived virtually unchanged for centuries. Accounting truly is the universal language of business.

CHAPTER 4

The Three Rules of Accounting

(That Business Owners Must Know)

There are three inviolable rules that apply to the use of accounting in a small business. Many small business owners do not know these rules—perhaps because they have never been told about them, but more likely because they have not understood how important accounting is to the running of a business.

These rules are not engraved in stone and were not handed down to me from on high. Rather, they represent a distillation of what I believe to be fundamental truths about accounting and its role in business planning, operations, and management.

In developing these rules, I've had to hack away some of the myths that have grown up around accounting, its application, and its function. These myths include the belief that accounting is an arcane black art to be practiced and understood only by trained professionals—numerical alchemists—and the idea that if the accounts are materially accurate they're fine. While these myths enjoy some currency in the minds of many small business owners, the three rules dispel them.

In this chapter, we will look at those three rules.

Rule 1: Accounting Is Black and White.

Big public companies have a lot of complex accounting decisions to make that generally involve compliance rules for the SEC and reporting requirements put in place by governmental agencies.

Most small businesses, on the other hand, do not have to report to governmental agencies except on taxes. In this book, I am not referring to our ever-changing world of tax accounting, which is governed by tax law as interpreted by the tax authorities. Tax accounting is often characterized as "compliance"—that is, adherence to governmental regulations. In tax accounting, much is gray and open to interpretation. Your CPA can help you with tax accounting.

Accounting for business operations, which is the subject of this book, is for the most part not for the government. It is for you, the business owner. It is a tool to make sure that you have the good information needed for making sound business decisions.

Owning a business requires solving problems with a multitude of judgment calls. The toughest problems are never clear, and obvious answers are as extinct as the dodo. Often a situation presents itself in which there are two good options, but limited resources allow for the pursuit of only one of them. A more challenging situation is when a multitude of options are present and they all look bad.

"I'll try the less bad option, please."

Accounting is one of the few things in life that are black and white. There's no guesswork. The treatment of every transaction and the resulting calculations are either right or wrong. If business owners can figure out the right answers, they will be following the map to success.

"That may be true for some things," many business owners will say, "but my business is different." No, it is not. All businesses today are simply derivations of other businesses that have been around for centuries. The technology has changed, the service has changed, the product has changed, people's attitudes have changed, the people needed to do the job have changed, the environment has changed, the politics and laws have changed, but the accounting…

Remarkably, the accounting has not changed, as we discussed in the previous chapter. In the 1400s, one of history's most powerful families, the Medicis, traded spices for gold, and the accounting entries were the same as today when Facebook trades page views for advertising dollars. When Al Capone traded liquor for guns in the 1930s, his bookkeeper accounted for the entries in a ledger book the exact way that a start-up yoga studio accounts for class fees and yoga instructor payments in Quickbooks. Today, when GE delivers locomotive engines to Burlington Northern, its accounts receivable and collection process is accounted for the same way as a local law firm's.

This concept is both frightening and stress relieving. It is frightening that something in business has not changed in over five hundred years. On the other hand, it is nice to know that there are some things we can depend on to be right and wrong.

Rule 2: Always Use Accrual-Based Accounting.

Accrual-based accounting will give you an accurate picture of where your business's operations stand at any time.

Under accrual-based accounting, **revenue** is recognized when it is earned.

Many businesses invoice their customers. Some receive payments and deposits with a sale before they deliver their products or services; others receive payments after they have delivered. Some businesses are paid in trade, and others, unfortunately, never get paid. None of this matters when considering when to record revenue for the business.

The only thing that matters in accounting is: When did the business earn the money?

When the money is earned (meaning when the business has a legal right to it)—then and only then does the business record the revenue. There may be long discussions of when the revenue is earned, but those are business discussions. In accounting, the minute the revenue is earned it is accounted for and put into the accounting records.

Consider the following example.

Johnny is in the public relations business. He sells consulting services and helps other businesses market themselves to the press. He is growing the business rapidly and has a goal of one day selling the business to a nationwide advertising agency.

When I reviewed his financial statements, he had about $500,000 a month in sales. Customer payments, however, fluctuated. The business received $300,000 one month and $700,000 another month. Some people paid early, some paid late, some paid on time, and some never paid. Collections varied from month to month, and that's normal in a business.

However, in this business, the business owners were accounting for the revenue when they received the customers' payments. That's called cash-basis accounting.

They had a baseline of costs of about $500,000 every month, which seemed reasonable. Their income statement showed their revenue fluctuating from $300,000 in March to $700,000 in June. That led them to think, "Wow, that was a bad March, but June looks great! What did we do differently in June?" They concluded that these financial results must be because most of the clients had a June fiscal year-end.

However, this conclusion was incorrect. The revenue disparities on their books were the result of recording revenue when the company received cash from customers. Accrual-based accounting (instead of cash-based) would have shown that their sales were the same in March as in June: $500,000 each, not $300,000 in one and $700,000 in the other.

This inaccurate accounting had consequences. From this incorrect data, Johnny decided to beef up his marketing spending the next year in April and May to try to get more business in the June contracting cycle. Unfortunately, this strategy yielded results no different than his other marketing, and it cost him considerable amounts of cash.

When the marketing results came back the same as the previous year, Johnny had a new problem: He was extremely busy for a short period but now lacked the budget to market for the rest of the year. He stopped taking a salary and fired a couple of key employees due to the new-found lumpiness in his workload, cash flow, and revenue.

Have you ever made a bad decision because of information you received from a reliable source that turned out to be…not so reliable?

Accounting for revenue when it is earned is the only way that your revenue numbers will be reliable.

The other side of the profit and loss statement is the **expenses**. These are things that take money out of the business.

Have you ever paid in advance for something (like insurance) for the full year? Have you ever received something (a product or service) and paid for it only after you got it? Expenses, like revenue, are recorded in the books only when they are incurred. It does not matter when they were paid for or when a product was ordered. The only thing that matters is when you incurred the expense.

If you have ever used an attorney, you know the frustration in getting their bills. The bills often lack description, are sent out late, do not include the detailed hours, and fail to provide their hourly rates. To ensure that you are looking at accurate business performance, the key question for your legal service expense is: When were the legal services performed? If the answer is September, then those legal services are a September expense. It does not matter that you got the invoice in October; the only thing that matters is that you received the service in September, and therefore that was when the expense was incurred.

Similarly, even though a business pays for its annual industry membership for the year in January, it only incurs expense for the membership in the month it received the benefit of that organization (in this case every month out of the year). Therefore, a $12,000 membership bill paid for in January for the whole year's worth of benefits shows only $1,000 worth of expense in January, $1,000 worth of expense in February, and so on throughout the year.

Consider the case of Jim, who appeared to have had a very bad January.

"January looks terrible," the accountant told the owner. "What is happening? Does your business go in cycles like that?"

"No," Jim said. "In fact, we tend to get a lot of new orders in January after the government budgets are freed up in the fall."

"But it looks as if your expenses are 50 percent higher in January than any other month," the accountant pointed out. "What's going on? What happens in January?"

"That's just the way January has always been for us," he said. "It has always been a terrible month."

The accountant probed a little deeper, trying to find out what it was about January that made it appear to be a "bad" month.

"Well, first, I have to pay these massive insurance premiums, and I am in the construction business. Insurance premiums for me are half a million dollars for the year, and I pay them all in January."

"How do you handle that problem?" the accountant asked.

"I've got it kind of figured out now. I reduce prices in January so that I can get more sales and more deposits in. Last year I broke even in January because I cut prices 9 percent across the board for anyone who signed and gave me a deposit right away."

Not a bad idea in itself—Jim was trying to solve a cash flow problem by cutting prices, thereby decreasing profit but increasing cash flow. Unfortunately, this solution was based on a misdiagnosis of the problem.

When the accountant dug into the issue, she found that Jim had not assessed *where his business stood,* because he was not accounting for the insurance premiums on the accrual basis. Just because he paid those premiums in January did not mean the total amount of premiums was an expense for January. After all, if he had canceled that insurance policy in February, he would have received a huge refund, because he would only have used one month's worth of insurance. The correct way to account for that expense is to spread it over the entire year.

If Jim had accounted for it that way, he never would have lowered prices; he would have seen that his business was profitable every single month. Accrual-based accounting would have shown him that his business was working correctly even though his cash cycle was challenging.

When he lowered prices, unfortunately he cut them past the point of profitability for the projects. In fact, when his accountant did a study, it was clear that he would have lost money even by lowering prices only 4.7 percent. At 9 percent, it was taking him all the way through May to recoup the losses from his January discounting.

Jim was accounting for things on a cash basis, which led him to make a poor pricing decision—and he did not even see it, because he was using incorrect accounting methods. By operating his business based on cash instead of accrual, he lost a third of the year's profits. Worse, he had been doing it for years.

If expenses are not properly accrued, the company's results can be misinterpreted. Bill's chocolate business, for example, lost $100,000 over the first six months of the year. Then, in the second half of the year, it made $200,000, so he is up $100,000 for the year. What does he automatically think? He must have done something better in the second half!

What are the ways an owner can improve a business's performance? Sales could go up, but let's assume Bill's sales were flat. Most business owners look at the bottom line, so Bill might look at the second half of the year and say, "Yeah, my sales were flat but I made $200,000. So expenses must have gone down."

Now let's look at what really happened in this situation. In the second half of the year, Bill moved his business to an office that gave him four months of "free rent" for signing a five-year lease. Under accrual-based accounting principles, which focus on the true economic costs of operating a business, he should not account for "free rent" by recording zero cost in his rent account. Instead, the entire amount of rent that's due over the course of the lease should be prorated over all the months of the lease, and that prorated monthly amount recorded as an expense every single month. So even during a "free rent" period, his expenses would show that he was incurring rent expense.

Bill's accounting was showing that he was not paying rent. But he was not operating rent-free—he had just been given a rent abatement. The total rent remained the same over the course of the lease. While his books showed that he had done well in the second half of the year, all he had done was not pay rent. He had not done anything to improve business operations, and that became clear the next year.

In January, he started losing money again because he no longer had the "free rent." He rationalized: "Well, that's normal, because last year I lost money in January, too. I'll just wait for the back half of the year. Things will be better, just as they were last year." But, of course, that did not happen, and the books reflected that because the actual rent payments were being recorded as expenses. Bill lost an entire year's worth of time (and ability) to solve his larger business issues. Instead, he was fooled into believing he would be okay based on bad data from his accounting department. At this point, his business could run out of cash and fail.

If Bill had had an accurate understanding of the company's expenses, he would have had a much better chance of saving the business. He might have pushed to make sales. He might have dropped a product line that was unprofitable. He might have increased prices for enhanced margins. He might have tried to sell more to his existing customers. He might have negotiated with his suppliers to try to get better gross margins. There was a myriad of possible solutions.

When a business is losing money, the owner is motivated to change things. When a business is making money, the owner is not quite so motivated. The worst-case scenario is when a business owner is lulled into believing the business is profitable when it is not. If owners are not making money in their business, they need to know that right away so that they can do something about it.

Without accrual-based accounting, owners are blind (or worse, fooled). Accrual-based accounting will open your eyes and let you see the truth of how your business is operating, and you may find that the figures you have been relying on are dangerously misleading. Generally, business owners have great intuition. They have a feel for what is going on with their business. They are smart, hardworking, and motivated. For many business owners, it is better to do nothing and not look at any financial statements than to rely on one that's misleading.

It is like having the wrong map. The other week I was heading to a meeting, and Apple Maps had me spinning in circles on the wrong side of the street. Ultimately, I had to look at the building numbers myself and assess the situation, course-correct, and figure it out myself.

If you have no map, your sense of direction might still get you to the destination. If you are relying on the wrong map, you are going to be in trouble. Do not be left wandering in the business woods with the wrong map.

By using inaccurate accounting methods, one in twenty small businesses do exactly that and wind up horribly lost. Many of these owners don't use their financial statements to make decisions, but some do. If you do not use accrual-based accounting and you are not matching the figures to the right period, then you are likely making assumptions that are wrong. This could lead you to pursue a disastrous course of action or business plan or decide not to do something that would correct a deficiency in your business operations.

Typically, when people are accounting for their revenue incorrectly, they are also accounting for their actual product costs incorrectly. The business owner thinks, "I bought a lot of product in January, so that's why my January costs were so high." That's the wrong way to look at these costs—it is a cash-based way of accounting for the cost. In fact, if an owner bought a lot of product and is going to resell it, the cost of the product is an investment in inventory, not a cost.

Once the product is sold and out the door, then the owner should record the cost of that product as a cost of goods sold. Until then, however, it is an investment in inventory that is an asset waiting to be sold. It is something of value that the owner possesses.

Cash-basis accounting has a beguiling simplicity. As shown in the previous examples, however, it will often provide an inaccurate, unreliable, and even misleading picture of how your business is operating in a real economic sense. In contrast, accrual-based accounting is based on the economic realities of your business.

Accrual-based books will give you a sound basis for gauging the profitability of individual products, various lines of business, various business units, and the entire business. Accurate accounting will bring into sharp focus expenses that should be cut or inefficiencies that can be improved. Most importantly, it will give you the peace of mind that comes from having a trustworthy picture of where you are, how you got there, where you are going, and how you can hit your goals.

Rule 3: Accounting Needs to Be Done by More Than One Person.

This third rule deals with how to implement your accounting system. You should always use at least two people in your accounting processes. You may have some concerns about following this rule. For example, you might ask, "Why should my accounting be done by more than one person? My business is not that complicated. What's the harm in using one person to do my accounting? What benefits will result if I use two people?" All good questions. As you'll see, the reasons for this rule are to ensure accuracy, enhance the speed and usefulness of financial reports, save on overall accounting costs, and eliminate fraud.

Financial statements are useful only if they are *accurate*. We all strive to do our best, but we inevitably fall short. Even if I hire the most amazing CFO on the planet to do all my accounting work, at some point that person will make a mistake. Everyone does. Have you ever sent an email with a misspelling or typo, despite having proofread it repeatedly? It can happen to anyone. It can be difficult to discover, let alone own up to, our own mistakes.

So how do you get accurate and reliable accounting records? By having one person who is knowledgeable in accounting check the work that has been done by another person. That's how you eliminate mistakes inside your financial statements to the greatest extent possible. And having financial statements that are uncorrupted by mistakes is critical if you are going to use those statements as the basis for business decisions. Mistakes inside your financial statements will invariably lead to the wrong place: wrong conclusions and bad decisions.

Speed in preparing internal financial statements is an issue that will resonate with a lot of people. Business owners should look at their financial statements no later than the fifteenth of the following month. Why is that important? Because if they are not seeing the financial statements until the twenty-fifth, they could lose opportunities to correct mistakes. By that point, a mistake might have been repeated. By getting the financial statements earlier in the month, owners can save time, energy, and money.

How would you like to compete in a twelve-mile race where all your competitors got a one-mile head start? That is what is happening if you allow your accounting department to get you financial statements after the fifteenth. You are in business to win, achieve your mission, and fulfill your goals. You cannot do that if you are constantly one month behind.

Another benefit of timely accounting is peace of mind. The faster you get the numbers, the less you have to stress about where you ended up, and the more confidence you will have in your ability either to make improvements or to continue on a successful path.

If you have only one accountant, he or she has to reconcile every account alone, one by one. If you have a bookkeeper, accounting manager, and controller, they can reconcile the accounts in tandem. When you can get things done simultaneously, as opposed to one by one, you get to the finish line a lot faster. Further, the expertise achieved by each accountant focusing on particular aspects of the accounting process will, over time, lead to enhanced efficiencies in producing the financial statement on a timely basis.

Cost efficiency is the third reason that accounting needs to be done by more than one person. In my experience, small businesses either overspend or underspend dramatically on their accounting. One owner, for instance, may use a $1,000-a-month bookkeeper, underspending and getting inaccurate work that isn't timely, while another hires a full-time controller or CFO, spending $7,000 to $30,000 a month. While that person may be providing accurate information, it may be more than is needed to operate the business efficiently.

If the accounting functions are staffed at the right level, however, business owners will spend a lot less money. One can have the bookkeeper doing bookkeeping duties and an accounting manager reconciling complex balance sheet items, while a controller does the fore-casting and projections and the CFO advises on strategic business issues. As a small business owner, you need very little CFO time in the course of a month or a year, but you do need a lot of bookkeeping time. Who is cheapest? The bookkeeper, of course—but you need a CFO, or you will miss out on the types of opportunities that an astute CFO can find.

For cost efficiency, you need to tier the work at the right levels at the right time—in other words, pay people at the level of what they are doing and their expertise. If you have your CFO reconciling your bank account, you are wasting money. Conversely, if you have your bookkeeper trying to do forecasting and projections, you are also wasting money because the information likely will be wrong and therefore unreliable. You might as well have not paid for it at all.

The conventional wisdom is that a business should use a book-keeper until it achieves $10 million in revenue, and at that point it should hire a controller; it should hire a CFO when it gets to $20 million or $25 million. However, a blended hybrid scenario may also make sense for some small businesses. Using a mix of full-time personnel to do the basic job of keeping the books, and part-time consultants to prepare the financial statements and provide expertise in interpreting them, is likely best for this situation. Each business will have its own unique needs, and the accounting function should be staffed appropriately to reflect those needs.

The bottom line is that a fully functioning, accurate accounting department should cost somewhere between 1 and 3 percent of a business's total revenues. This is a wide variance, but it is important to note that a single-product wholesale operation requires simple accounting and should cost no more than 1 percent of revenue. On the opposite side of the spectrum, a manufacturing firm with hundreds of products and thousands of parts with complex machinery is probably going to spend closer to 3 percent of revenue to get accurate accounting.

Elimination of Fraud

Catching fraud is not the focus of my business, but I am devoting a good portion of this chapter to the topic to emphasize that it is a real problem and that good accounting and best practices are the only way to battle it.

The Society of Certified Fraud Examiners, a national group, publishes an annual survey on fraud—in particular for small businesses, which the group defines as those that bring in under $100 million in revenue. Last year, the society reported that fraud was occurring in about 28.8 percent of all small businesses. Those are reported cases of intentional fraud. Those are people who are willing to raise a hand and say, "Yes, someone stole from me." The latest data indicate that the loss from fraud is about $154,000, on average, per occurrence.

To put this in perspective, if a business has a 10 percent net margin, it needs $1,540,000 in new sales just to recoup the lost fraud dollars. Worse, if it wants to make up for the lost profit, it needs to make an additional $3,080,000 in new sales to make up for an average-size fraud. The business not only needs to make up for the original loss but also the wasted time it took to replace the profit.

If I told you I just sold $3,080,000 worth of your product or service for you today, you would probably kiss me and pay me a ton of money. Eliminate fraud and you have just saved yourself an extra $3 million in sales.

Unfortunately, if one person is doing everything in the accounting department, then the door is wide open to fraud. The person who steals might not have started out as a bad person, but he or she has all the control and is the only one seeing things. If a business provides the temptation for theft by not implementing the proper controls, it will be stolen from. The statistics prove that theft can happen in a number of ways—and without someone else watching, most of those ways are virtually undetectable.

My experience has brought to light a number of ways an ethically challenged employee can defraud a business. A few of these follow, just to illustrate the pervasiveness of this issue.

A manufacturing company came to my firm with a problem. It had good revenue—about $40 million a year—and seemed to be doing quite well, but it was losing money. Management felt the company did not have enough cash and might miss payroll or go out of business. We were hired do their accounting in an effort to figure out if there was a way to save the business.

Typically, when engaged by a client, our first order of business is to reconcile all the accounts to make sure we know our starting point. One of the balance sheet accounts is **payroll**. If a business owes people salaries or bonuses, the owner wants to make sure that's correct. If it owes people paid time off or vacation time, the owner wants to make sure that's accurate in order to get an accurate picture of the health of the business. To do that, we take the records from the company handling payroll (in this case, ADP) and match them up with what is in the accounting system.

When we did that for this client, we saw that the payroll number was high. We asked, "Has anybody ever reconciled the time sheets with the payroll numbers being submitted to the payroll company?" It turned out that nobody had ever done that. The current controller was very busy and never had the time to get around to that reconciliation.

In this particular manufacturing firm, there was a lot of overtime. That resulted in a $20 an hour employee, for example, becoming a $30 an hour employee, which had a substantial impact on profitability. We looked for cost savings anywhere we could. "Let's take a look at the time sheets," we said. "Where can we cut our overtime expense?"

When we dug into the payroll records, we found those records showed that five employees, one of whom was a supervisor, were all working, amazingly, in two separate locations that were a couple of miles apart at the same exact time on the same exact days. They must have been very hard workers!

The five culprits started off small. This is very typical of fraud. They started off cheating on one hour or two hours at a time. By the end, however, they were cheating on whole days. When they calculated their total number of hours, the payroll system automatically figured overtime. The company was paying them overtime on all the hours that they were supposedly spending at both jobs at the same time. They got away with it once; then they got away with it twice; and then it became a brazen way of life.

This was a company that had not reconciled payroll, because the controller did not have the time. The way it had staffed its accounting department was a fundamental problem—it had a controller and a bookkeeper and nobody in between. The bookkeeper was overwhelmed with too much to do in too little time, and the controller was also overwhelmed. The company lacked an accounting department staffed appropriately for its size. The work just wasn't getting done. It took time to dig this out, but it was well worth it. For almost three years, the company had not caught what these five employees were doing, and it was losing an average of $280,000 a year.

Having the accounting department appropriately staffed also enables business owners to build in processes. This company lacked an accounting process. It had no checklist of things that had to be done every month before the books could be closed. Stephen Covey, in his book *First Things First*, defines four quadrants for assessing the things that you do. They are either urgent or not urgent, and they are either important or unimportant. The things a lot of us get caught up doing are things that are urgent but not important. Rarely do we get to the things that are important but not urgent.

Reconciling payroll is incredibly important but doesn't seem urgent for anyone other than maybe an accountant. It is best to reconcile payroll monthly, for most companies, and at least quarterly for small businesses.

The important point is to have multiple people looking at the numbers, because then you have a better chance of catching problems earlier. This company's bookkeeper was not bad, nor was their controller. They were just overwhelmed and were not following a rigorous procedure. Instead, they were letting the work dictate how they got things done. If there was a fire, they had to put it out. If something had to be negotiated, it had to be negotiated immediately. There was no checklist or set of checks and balances to ensure that everyone was getting the most important things done.

Another common type of fraud is **double check writing**. One such case that made the news involved the bookkeeper for a pizza shop that did a few million in revenue a year. In this case, the bookkeeper managed to steal $530,000 over three years.

How did she do it? She was writing double checks. This is a common fraud, and pulling it off just requires a little alone time and a simple adjustment in the accounting software. In this particular case, the business owner thought he was doing everything correctly.

He was the only person allowed to sign checks. He had an annual review of the books by an independent accounting firm. He had a banker friend review his financials monthly and strategize with him on ways to make the business more profitable, and he had a separate CPA firm doing his taxes.

Unfortunately, the business, it appeared, was never quite profitable enough: It seemed to be leaking money, and everything was just too expensive. The food was great and the place was packed, but they just couldn't seem to make any money consistently.

The shop's reputation was growing, and the business owner took a second mortgage out on his house to keep the doors open. He was confident that he could make this business profitable, but if the business failed, he would lose his house. As luck would have it, he had known the bookkeeper for twenty years; she was his top employee who handled all sorts of things. She was hard working, supremely organized, always there, dependable, and loyal (or so he thought).

So when the bookkeeper got into a bad car accident, the business owner was extremely worried. He went to see her in the hospital and helped her son get to and from school from grandma's house. Almost immediately, he was forced to bring in a temporary bookkeeper to pay the bills, reconcile the accounts, etc., and that's when the original bookkeeper got caught.

How did she steal over $500,000 in three years? She started with a basic bill—a utility bill, for example—approved by the business owner and paid by check. In this case she would write one check to the utility company for the bill, perhaps $3,124 a month. She would then write another check to herself for $300. She would forge the second check and reconcile the bank account, and on the income statement it would show as $3,424, which looks "close."

Unfortunately, the bookkeeper was doing this same scheme across multiple expense categories: $300 in this category, $50 in that one, and maybe $600 in another, larger category. Over three years, all of the double checks amounted to $530,000, or about $15,000 per month.

Trying to cover her fraud, she would go into the accounting system and change the payee after the check was cut. That way, it looked as though there were really two checks going every month to the utility company—which, again, would be odd. But it is hard to catch (the auditors did not catch it), because it seems like about the right amount to pay each month. The owner of the pizzeria, even if he were inclined to look at the books, would say, "I guess that's about right. That's what it usually is."

Again, there was no accountability there. She was the only person working in the accounting department, and she alone wrote checks and reconciled the bank account. In my experience, that's not unusual. Most small businesses have one or maybe two accountants in their accounting department. Often, one person does it all. That's a structure that is ripe for fraud. Segregation of duties is critical. A business also needs clear job descriptions for each person and a process by which they do their work.

In the end, the pizza business was saved, but the owner did have to sell his house to pay off some debts. Hopefully, with a few good years under his belt, he will be able to buy another, better home; but for now, he is renting a condo for his family and working day and night to make amazing pizza profitable.

Accounting processes must be automatic in their application. That's not to say that a machine could do them but that the system and process needs to be exactly the same every time. One example is the accounts payable process. A business must have a process with separate sign-offs. When a bill comes in from a utility company, there is a checklist of steps to take to get that bill paid. The steps can be developed by asking questions about the process. For example, who signs off that the bill can be paid? Who signs the checks? Who reconciles the bank account? These duties should be handled by different people. If one person approves the expense, and another cuts the check, and another matches up the invoice to the check, you have a process that is pretty much impenetrable. It's hard for temptation to be acted upon under those conditions.

Another situation, this time involving **inventory**, came to my attention that highlights the importance of segregating accounting duties. In this case, the COO was responsible for going to the warehouse and counting the inventory. He would count the pallets and multiply the number by their cost to figure the company's monthly investment in inventory. The reason for doing this was to match the purchases and sales of goods with the beginning and ending inventory to make sure they reconciled. If, for example, the company started with zero inventory and then bought ten pallets and sold three, there should be seven remaining at the end of the month.

For two consecutive months, the COO reported a number of remaining pallets of inventory that did not match the company's accounting records. For example, he would report that four remained when the company's accounting system showed there should be six. When told his figures were wrong, he conceded that, yes, he had miscounted. Each time he recounted, his new number matched the accounting system number. That type of error might happen once, but when it recurs, you must investigate whether the inventory was "rigged."

The facts raised a red flag. The CEO was advised to have somebody else count the inventory. When the CEO explained this to the COO, the COO became defensive. He blamed the messenger, insisting the accounting was faulty.

After the third month in which the COO reported inventory that did not match the accounting records, a third-party accountant went with the COO to count the pallets of inventory. It turned out that even fewer pallets remained than the COO had reported.

When pressed, he blamed the inaccurate inventory count on waste associated with the previous month's jobs. In fact, there hadn't been any waste for many months—and the inventory was down $60,000 from where it should have been according to the accounting records.

The good news is that accounting is black and white, and there are really only two answers to this mystery. Either someone did not buy as much inventory as they had claimed and pocketed some money, or someone took some of the inventory after it had been bought. There are no other answers. If someone bought ten pallets and sold four, they should have had six in the warehouse. Ten minus four equals six. This is the beauty of accounting. It is not algebra. It is simple arithmetic.

As it turns out, the COO was selling inventory out the back door and doing jobs on the side. A quick investigation uncovered the details, but proper accounting found the theft. Had the accounting been incorrect, this might have gone on for months.

You need the right operations, processes, and procedures. You can eliminate fraud, theft, and waste. If you have the right systems and processes, you'll be able to easily detect and deter employee theft.

In addition, your organization as a whole will be more accountable. When you set the tone in the accounting that you will not tolerate theft, you are also communicating the message "We expect everybody to do their job correctly, and you will be held accountable."

Excessive use of supplies can also indicate employee theft, but to determine whether usage is excessive, you need to **benchmark** your business. Let me explain. A company asked us to implement our process, and one of the things we did was to benchmark their office supplies to what would be typical in the industry. We found the company was using three times the typical amount of office supplies for a company their size in their industry.

In this case, the company had almost no overhead and no real paper. Its office supplies should have cost around $200 a month, $300 a month maximum. We found, however, that the office supply expenses were up to $900 a month.

This anomaly caught our attention, and we began our work by matching up the receipts with expenses. All the receipts looked okay. We asked the office manager to show us the storeroom where the paper was kept.

The records showed the company had bought twenty reams of paper, but only four of them were in the storeroom.

The office manager explained the disparity by claiming the company had just had a big paper project. But the nature of the firm was that it did not need to use much paper. We looked at the industry average, and the monthly cost should have been closer to $250.

As it turned out, the office manager was buying extra office supplies from a store, then taking them back and getting a gift card. Then she used the gift card to buy something for less than the gift card amount so that she could get the rest back as cash. This had been happening for months. It took a second set of eyes armed with industry benchmarking data to ferret out this fraud.

Although small, this saved the company about $7,000 per year; more importantly, it showed that management was carefully watching all of the expenses in the business.

The lesson here, once again, is that numbers matter greatly, and business owners need to pay attention to them. That's how a company can weed out fraud. Catching fraud is by no means all that a good accounting department can do. A great accounting department finds waste, overspending, and underutilization of resources; highlights those issues; and helps build a plan to solve the underlying problems.

CEOs and business owners focus a tremendous amount of energy on getting new sales and sometimes fail to look at expenses as one of the first lines of defense. As discussed before, for every dollar of theft prevented, and for every dollar of expense saved, it is $20 less that the business has to sell to make the same amount of money if it has a 10 percent net profit margin.

How do you set up a proper accounting department?

In a small business, where the business cannot afford more than a simple bookkeeper (these are typically businesses with less than $2 million in annual revenue), the owner must have a CPA looking over the shoulder of the person doing the books. I suggest letting your bookkeeper know that one month out of the year (and make it a surprise) you are going to have your CPA or other outside firm come in and run the books.

Ask the bookkeeper to establish rigorous process documents and procedures for this outside firm to follow. Just the simple threat of an outside firm looking into the deepest parts of the accounting files will both increase performance and decrease your risk of fraud.

In a better scenario, a business would staff its accounting department with two different people with different skill levels doing the books at different levels. These individuals need to be cross-trained to ensure continuity in the event that one quits, is fired, or becomes disabled. Then, for at least two months out of each year, each accountant needs to do the other's job. Once again, make this random and require rigor in documentation and process.

In these fraud stories, the businesses were filing taxes, which means the CPAs were looking at the files every year. The larcenous employees were able to hide the fraud from the company's CPAs. This fact illustrates that it is generally not enough just to have a CPA prepare your tax return.

Here's my best-case recommendation for staffing your accounting needs. A *bookkeeper* should do the data entry. A part-time accountant, the *accounting manager*, should oversee that person and do more complex reconciliations. Another part-time accountant, the *controller*, should oversee the accounting manager and do forecasting and projections on where the business is going. Finally, you should have a part-time *CFO* who is overseeing the department and providing strategic advice. This way, you have a tiered system of oversight, and each level is policing the other three levels.

If you have four people's eyes on a set of financials, and your CPA looks at them every year as well, you have near zero chance of fraud—unless all four people, plus your CPA, are in on the fraud from day one.

Accurate accounting promotes accountability. Having accurate financials also brings peace of mind. Accurate accounting offers business owners the reassurance that they are profitable, increasing cash flow, and growing the business value; as a result, they can sleep better at night. By doing the accounting correctly with the right staffing and the right process, business owners get the peace of mind of knowing that the ethically challenged employee's larcenous tendencies will be thwarted.

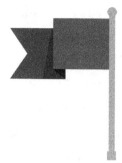

CHAPTER 5

The Triple Bottom Line

When I visit the doctor, there are three measurements or readings the nurse always takes: temperature, pulse, and blood pressure. These three measurements—my vital signs—quickly show whether there is a problem with my health and point to the nature of that problem. Based on these vital signs, the doctor can determine a course of treatment or whether more tests are needed.

Businesses also have three key vital signs, which I call the Triple Bottom Line: net operating income, net cash from operations, and net equity.

Chapters 6 and 7 will deal with the details of those three vital signs. First, though, let's do some groundwork by defining some key concepts and take a look at how analyzing the Triple Bottom Line will reveal the health of your business for any given month.

Reading each of these bottom lines is fairly straightforward. If all of them are going up, then life and your business's health are good. If one of the three is going down, you have a problem that requires attention.

Net operating income (NOI) is a company's income after operating expenses have been deducted but before income taxes and interest are deducted. The NOI is, in effect, a measurement of how well you are running your business. Defined in a way that would make all seventh-grade English teachers cringe, your net operating income is the net income you get from operating your business.

It is not the income you get from winning the lottery. It is not the income you get from winning (or lose from losing) a lawsuit. It is not income derived from the sale of a piece of equipment (unless your business *is* the sale of equipment). It is not the income you lose when you have to pay for one-time extraordinary expenses. It also is not the income you gain when you charge late fees or interest. It is only the income you receive from your normal business operations.

Many people confuse net operating income with EBITDA (earnings before interest, taxes, depreciation, and amortization). However, because depreciation (for most businesses) is an operating expense, any depreciation costs shown in the financials will represent a more accurate picture of the costs associated with running the business.

It is fine to define the value of the business by its EBITDA, but you are fooling yourself if you think the million-dollar machine you just purchased won't wear out and require repairs. EBITDA is also a widely accepted measurement for free cash flow. However, EBITDA is a dangerous management metric because it does not provide a clear understanding of the true costs (cash or cashless) that it takes to run the business.

Cash from operations is the cash you receive from operating your business. It is not the cash you receive from a bank loan, or an equity investment, or the sale of a piece of real estate. It is your company's cash flow as measured by net income, adjusted for the month change in your operating balance sheet accounts (things like accounts receivable, accounts payable, prepaid expenses, and deferred revenue). Those adjustments will fluctuate depending on whether customers are paying you now or later and on whether you are paying suppliers now or later. Cash from operations will reveal how well you are managing cash and is perhaps the single most important short-term metric: Are your business operations bringing more money in than is going out, or are you making a lot of money but never seem to have enough cash?

Net equity is the measure of a company's financial strength. Net equity measures a business's financial ability to withstand tough times. How well prepared is your business for the next economic downturn?

Do you think we are going to be in a recession in the next seven to ten years? Statistically speaking, it is guaranteed. Whatever the case, there are only three situations that you may find yourself in during the next recession. First, your business may fail. Second, like some of the stronger businesses in your industry, it may survive. Third, like very few of the businesses in your industry, your company may take advantage of the economic situation to grow market share, customer profitability, new assets, new markets, and new products. If you fall into this third category of business, you will dominate the competition and pray for a recession. As Warren Buffett says, "I love it when the market goes down, then I get to buy things that are on sale!"

Net equity measures how much a company owns, minus how much it owes. It is a very basic equation and another simple concept. It is not unlike the equity you might have in a house. Your net equity figure tells you the level of safety in your business. The more net equity, the stronger, and therefore safer, your company will be. Each month, this third component of the Triple Bottom Line will show whether your company got stronger or weaker.

How to Use the Triple Bottom Line

The three elements of the Triple Bottom Line provide vital signs of your business's health. They may not provide a complete diagnosis, but they will show if something is not quite right and whether more tests need to be run to get to the bottom of the problem and develop an effective course of treatment. Let's look at some scenarios where one of the three elements might be going down and what might be going on.

Scenario 1: When net operating income is up but cash from operations is down

Assume that the net operating income of Nancy's business is positive, and that net equity is up $50,000. But meanwhile the net cash from operations is down by $10,000. What might have happened?

Let's take a look. Nancy had $50,000 in net income for the month, increasing her balance sheet by $50,000. She has increased accounts receivable by $50,000, but if she did not collect any of it, she did not get any cash out of the sales. If she spent $50,000 on wages and to replenish her inventory, that would be a $50,000 decrease in cash. Because she did not collect any cash, her cash account would be $50,000 less than the balance at the end of the previous month. It might even be negative.

This is a common scenario in business, and it is the reason most business owners feel that they are doing well but are always out of cash. There are a number of things you and Nancy can do to fix this cash problem.

Thankfully, the use of the Triple Bottom Line gives Nancy the tools to see the problem. The next thing she must do is ask some hard questions:

- With our clients not paying, are we selling to the right customers?

- Are we selling the right product?

- Do we have the right terms in our contract (or are we the last to get paid)?

- Do we have the right accounting and billing processes?

Maybe Nancy is selling services to the government. She knows the government takes ninety days to pay, so that's part of our cash cycle, and that's okay.

Or maybe she is selling a product that's defective; she is accounting for the sales as they happen, but sixty days later her customers return the product. Or worse, maybe salespeople and the accounting department are inaccurately reporting sales that never really show up. That would be a big problem.

Maybe Nancy's sales contract is not good in its provisions for returns or allowances, or in some way allows people to not pay her. Could it be that her customers see that she charges no interest, late fees, or penalties and therefore would rather pay off their credit cards to avoid the 18 percent interest than pay her? In other words, are they borrowing money from her for free, knowing that delaying the payment is no big deal?

Maybe she has salespeople who are actually pitching these disincentives. Maybe she is paying her salespeople based on sales rather than collections. If so, is she incentivizing them to sell the wrong product to the wrong customers under the wrong terms just to get their commission? Is she letting some customers use her as a bank, even though she paid sales commissions to get them?

Does any of this sound like issues you are experiencing?

There are several possible business vampires that may be sucking the cash out of the business, but cash is a problem that Nancy needs to solve. Most businesses fail because they run out of cash. If your net income and net equity are up but nonetheless the cash from operations is decreasing month over month, then you immediately have to investigate, identify your cash vampires, and kill them. You must not run out of cash.

Scenario 2: When cash from operations is up but net operating income is down

Let's say the net cash from operations for Noah's business is up— perhaps he collects a lot of money from customers who decided to pay in December so they could get a tax break. Money flooded in in December, and because Noah did not pay out as much cash as he took in, net cash from operations is positive.

Meanwhile, his net operating income is down, which means his business did not make a profit. In this particular month, his business model has failed. He needs to know why and immediately. He should ask himself:

- Was my price wrong?

- Was my product wrong?

- Did I not sell enough?

- Were expenses too high?

- Where might I make cuts or add sales to get my net operating income back into positive territory?

But then Noah looks at the net equity figure, and he sees that it is up. How can net equity be up if net income is down?

Would the collection of all that cash have affected Noah's net equity? This is a common incorrect assumption made by management. Unfortunately for Noah, all he did was convert accounts receivable to cash, and accounts receivable was already an asset on the balance sheet.

For example, if Noah collects $200,000 of accounts receivable, he now has $200,000 of cash where he used to have $0, and he has $0 accounts receivable where he used to have $200,000. He still has the exact same amount of assets (just one went up and the other went down). So the collection of that cash did not impact net equity.

There must have been some third-party situation that came in to cause the rise in the net equity. If net equity went up at the same time that net operating income has declined, it generally means that shareholders put more money into the business as a contribution. That is one explanation as to why net operating income could be down while the figures for both the net equity and the net cash from operations could be up.

There are only two reasons net equity goes up in most small businesses:

1. Net operating income was positive.

2. Shareholders/owners contributed money to the business.

Scenario 3: When net equity is down but both net operating income and cash from operations are up

Now, consider what might be happening if the net equity of Nigel's business is the only one of the three elements of his Triple Bottom Line that is down. Both his net operating income and his net cash from operations are up.

If net operating income is up, Nigel gets the message, generally, that he is operating his business model in an appropriate way. And, if his net cash from operations is up, that means he did well in collecting his money and not spending it before he got it. And yet, his net equity dropped and the business became weaker. This is a silent killer of small businesses.

Net equity going down while net operating income and cash from operations are up is a scary scenario that happens quite often in privately held businesses—and it is one of the key factors leading to the failure of a good business.

Net equity only goes down for two reasons:

1. Net income was negative—meaning the company lost money.

2. Owners are taking money out of the business.

For Nigel, he did well last year. Profits were up 20 percent. Sales were up 18 percent, and his business was executing to happy customers. He bought a new house for the family six months ago, he needed more money than he thought for the renovations this year, and he increased a few of his other personal expenses.

This year, Nigel's income at his business declined about 7 percent from the previous year, but the business is still doing well. There are plans for a sales increase, and Nigel believes he is going to get the business back on track. The real reason for the decrease is that one of Nigel's main salesmen is not hitting his numbers. But, Nigel thinks to himself, it could be a lot worse—at least income is only down 7 percent.

Unfortunately, without realizing it, that small 7 percent change in net income means that Nigel is now taking out more cash than the company's profits after tax.

In the previous scenario, remember, Noah's net equity went up even while the net income was going down. The explanation was that the owner or shareholders were contributing money into the business. It can go the other way, and it often does—as it has for Nigel.

Nigel has a big mortgage payment, a big car payment, and other personal expenses that come to $10,000 for the month, but he only makes $15,000 of net income in the business. That sounds fine... but it is not. The biggest creditor in your business is the IRS, and they want $7,000 of the $15,000 in tax. That means Nigel only has $8,000 left to spend. Nigel is $2,000 per month short.

But mortgage payments don't stop, and Nigel can't pull his kids out of private school. So, where is he going to get the extra $2,000?

He can pull it from the business—and then what happens? His net equity goes down, because he is taking out more money than he is making.

Business owners need to be very careful with this. Let's say you are making $20,000 a month in your business and you are spending $21,000. Net equity is going down just a trickle, $1,000 a month, but it is a silent, slow bleed that eventually could be fatal.

Many small businesses are what are called "pass-through entities." Those are S corporations, partnerships, LLCs, etc. In pass-through entities, there are only two ways that the owner can get money into the business. He or she can either lend it to the business or put it in as a contribution. With a contribution, the equity value of the business goes up by the amount of the contribution.

On the other side of the coin, there are only three ways that you, as a business owner, might get money out of your business. First, if you have lent money to the business you can repay yourself some of that loan principal. Second, you can take a salary (or guaranteed payment in an LLC). Third, you can take distributions. A distribution is simply a removal of cash out of the company to yourself, personally, as a shareholder. Distributions reduce the equity in your business, thereby making the business weaker and more susceptible to failure.

The bottom line is the Triple Bottom Line. The Triple Bottom Line provides quick and concise clarity and understanding without having to turn oneself into an accountant. The information contained in the Triple Bottom Line can give you remarkable insight, peace of mind, and positive motivation. With the newfound confidence and knowledge of the three elements contained in the Triple Bottom Line, you can increase the profitability, safety, security, and value of your business.

In the next two chapters, we will take a closer look at the three elements of the Triple Bottom Line.

CHAPTER 6

Net Operating Income and Your Business Model

Most people think of net income as their bottom line. They make money, they spend money, and what is left—or what they owe—is the bottom line. In large part that's correct, but net income by itself does not tell business owners much about the health of their business. It really just indicates at a high level whether their business is profitable, but it doesn't tell them whether it is operating at full strength. To do that, owners need to understand how their business performs in comparison to the business model for their industry.

Let me take a moment to explain what I mean by "business model." A business model represents the ideal metrics for a typical business in a given industry. Each of us has ideal metrics that are used in assessing our fitness given our height, weight, and age. For example, for a person who is forty years old, five-foot-ten, and 180 pounds, the ideal metrics might be a heart rate of sixty-two beats per minute and blood pressure of 110 over 70. With that information, if you are similar in age and size you can determine whether your heart rate and blood pressure are more or less than those standards and, in turn, what that means in terms of your fitness. Armed with that information, you can then take steps to improve those numbers and your fitness. You won't be merely surviving; you'll be fit and thriving.

For every type of business there are standards—expressed as percentages of top line revenue of the typical business in an industry—that can provide comparative diagnostic information. These metrics are the model against which business owners can judge the fitness of their business.

Let me demonstrate by giving examples of what a business model would look like for businesses in various industries.

Software Business

For a software business—i.e., one that develops, produces, and sells software products—the business model metrics would look like the following:

Revenue or sales	100%
Cost of goods sold (COGS)	(20%)
Gross profit/gross margin	80%
Sales, general, and administrative expenses (SG&A)	(50%)
Net operating income (NOI)	30%

Manufacturing Business

For a manufacturing business—i.e., one that manufactures somewhat unique goods from raw materials and sells them—the business model metrics would look like this:

Revenue or sales	100%
COGS	(60%)
Gross profit/gross margin	40%
SG&A	(26%)
NOI	14%

Retail Business

For a retail business—i.e., one that buys finished goods, marks them up, and sells them—the business model metrics would look like the following:

Revenue or sales	100%
COGS	(55%)
Gross profit/gross margin	45%
SG&A	(30%)
NOI	15%

Even within these broad categories, there can be fairly large swings in the business model. A business owner will want to know how well their business operated as compared with the business model. But business models vary from industry to industry, from market to market, and based on company size, and owners need to know which models apply to their business. A construction business might have gross margins that are lower than 20 percent. In a high-tech business that develops software, gross margins could be above 85 percent.

Those are very different numbers reflecting the business realities of different industries. A software firm requires a tremendous amount of sales and marketing. It also requires substantial research and development to design, develop, and produce products that work and that people will use. If you produce software that people won't buy, you can lose millions of dollars. In contrast, at a construction firm you only need a hammer and nails and you can do the job. Because of the low barrier to entry, the construction industry is incredibly competitive. That competition drives down the gross profit and thus gross margins to low levels.

An income statement (also known as a profit and loss statement, or P&L) is the financial statement that shows how well a business is operating compared to the model. Whether a company is in software, construction, or some other industry, its owner needs to understand that industry's ideal business model.

A business's income statement covers four main topics. First, at the top of the income statement is the amount of *revenue* or "money earned" by the business during the period. Second, the income statement shows *gross profit,* which is revenue minus cost of goods sold (COGS), and third, it shows *operating expenses,* otherwise known as "sales, general, and administrative" (SG&A)—what it costs to operate the business in terms of rent, administrative staff, paper, travel, marketing and sales, etc.

Fourth, the interaction of these three items produces *net operating income,* which is the first piece of the Triple Bottom Line. Net operating income shows you how you can increase gross margin and adjust your operating expenses to make more money. It gives a business owner the means to discover how to do better than his or her competitors.

Each of these categories is expressed on the income statement as a number, and, when each number is converted to a percentage of revenue, it becomes the basis of comparison to the business model applicable to the business.

This filtering of business metrics through those of the business model can be a powerful management tool. By making these comparisons of actual to ideal business performance, the management team can answer such basic questions as: Is the business making the profit it should? Can and should the business increase prices? Is it possible to reduce the cost of goods sold through different purchasing approaches or by more efficient manufacturing or service delivery?

Better still, comparing your business performance to others can help you focus on the appropriateness of various expenses. For example, do you have the right rent structure? Are you overstaffed? Are shipping costs too high? Do you need to increase commissions to incentivize sales personnel?

The Three Dials of the Income Statement

There are only three dials you can adjust in an income statement: revenue, COGS, and SG&A. The way you turn these dials can have a huge impact on your net operating income and the value of your business.

As discussed earlier, **revenue** is what you have **earned**. It is not the cash you have brought in. If you close a sale or complete a job so that you can say you earned the right to be paid, then you can record that as revenue.

Keep in mind, though, that revenue is not cash. If a construction business gets a new job and receives a $20,000 retainer before it starts, it has not earned that cash even though it is in the bank. It is only after the work is done that the business has earned it. On the other hand, a consultant who works for a client but does not get paid for two months still earned the income the day he or she performed the work.

Even though it's nice to collect the cash, you don't earn it at the time it's paid but instead when the task you're hired to do is completed. It is important for business owners to keep that straight so that they can match up income with expenses. Otherwise a business might appear to be doing badly when it is, in fact, doing just fine, or vice versa.

The same exact philosophy applies to expenses. Expenses are not accounted for in the books until they are incurred. You may have paid a $10,000 deposit for that trade show booth, but it is not an expense until you attend the trade show and get the use of that booth.

Without accounting for revenue and expenses correctly, management will fool itself into thinking the business is more profitable or less profitable than it actually is. This leads to bad decisions. Bad decisions cost money and time and significantly decrease the value of the business. Revenue and expenses are properly matched in the correct period when the business uses the accrual accounting method. This matching principle is the basis for accrual-based accounting. If you do not remember anything about accrual-based accounting except "I have to match up income and expenses," then you are ahead of the game.

The cost of goods sold (COGS) is the second key component of an income statement. COGS is the expense associated with providing goods and services to the customer. Said more plainly, COGS is the cost of what you sell. Every business sells something, and as the business owner you need to know what it costs to make your product or provide your service. Without this information, you are driving blind—it is impossible to know how to price your product or whether you are profitable on each sale. Proper accounting is the map to tell you where you are and where you are going.

For all businesses, there are only five things that go into COGS. Why only five, and why these five? My best answer to that question is "That's the rule, and it works." Accounting is beautifully simple. The rules are hundreds of years old. Once you learn them, you don't have to worry about relearning them.

Here are the five components of COGS:

Direct materials: Every business needs "direct materials," or the supplies required to build a product or deliver a service. A doughnut shop, for example, would need supplies such as flour, eggs, milk, and sugar.

Direct labor: What else do you need to make doughnuts? Unfortunately, doughnuts do not make themselves. You need people to shape them and bake them or fry them and whatever else it takes to produce a doughnut. That's called direct labor: the people who directly touch the doughnuts, doing the hands-on work.

Indirect labor: What about the people who manage those folks? Let's say we have thirty people making doughnuts. We might have one or two managers overseeing the production. Those managers are called indirect laborers. A manager may not ever be able to actually say, "I made a doughnut." The janitor can't say that, either; he or she, too, is an indirect laborer, as is anyone whose job is to support the people who make the product.

Manufacturing overhead: The next component of COGS is the space that is needed to make a product or provide a service. In the doughnut shop, that's the back end. It is not the front end where they sell the doughnuts under glass cases. It is where the people are actually mixing the dough and using the ovens. If, say, we rent a 10,000 square foot building, and 8,000 square feet is used for the manufacturing of the doughnuts, you can post 80 percent of your rental expense as an overhead allocation in calculating COGS. If your business does not manufacture anything, you do not have any manufacturing overhead expense.

In-bound freight: The most arcane of the five elements of COGS is called "in-bound freight." It is the money that it takes to get your product's ingredients or parts to you. For example, let's say the doughnut shop buys a hundred pounds of flour a day to be shipped to the shop. The shipping charge associated with getting the flour to the shop gets added to the cost of goods sold.

Shipping costs for outbound freight to deliver the doughnuts are not COGS. Inbound freight is required to get our doughnuts made. We do not depend on outbound freight for that purpose. We need outbound freight to sell our doughnuts. It can be hard for business owners to see the difference. Don't think about it. Memorize it. It's the rule, and it has been this way for hundreds of years.

One caveat about outbound freight: If you mark up the freight or delivery charge for delivering your doughnuts, then you are providing delivery as a new service. You are now in the business both of making doughnuts and shipping doughnuts. So, if you pay $50 for the delivery of your doughnuts but charge $100, then the $100 is revenue and the $50 you spent on the freight is COGS associated with that revenue. Congratulations, you are in the freight business.

Sales, general, and administrative (SG&A) is the third component of the income statement. SG&A consists of everything that it takes to run and operate your business that's not in cost of goods sold.

It is easier to think of what does not go into SG&A than what does. There are only two things that do not go into SG&A: first, anything that goes into COGS, and second, any expense or income item that is not a part of "operating your business." The expenses or income items that are not directly associated with operations are called "other income or expense" items. Here are a few examples:

- Interest expense—Unless you are in the business of making loans to other people and using borrowed money to do it, interest costs in your business are a financing decision, not an operating decision. This is an important distinction. Today you may not be able to run your business without your loans and subsequent interest, but what if I were to give you all the money you needed to finance your business for 1 percent of the company—would you take it? Of course. If you take my deal, do you have any interest expense? Of course not. Interest expense therefore is not a product of your business model but rather a product of your decision on how to finance the business.

- One-time legal expenses—Unless you are in the business of suing people or being sued, one-time lawsuits and legal expenses are not a part of your business operations. Other than lawyers, no business sets out to get sued, yet many (if not most) businesses will be sued during their business life cycle. The expenses (and any winnings) associated with a lawsuit are therefore "other income" or "other expense" and not a part of SG&A.

- Sale of machinery—If you sell an asset like a piece of machinery or a vehicle, you will make or lose money. Unless you are in the machinery sales business, the income (or loss) you receive on the sale of the equipment is an "other income" or "other expense" item. You are not in the business of selling machinery, and therefore it is not a part of your SG&A.

- Any other one-time events or random activities, things that happened once, were not predicted to happen, or happened outside of the normal course of business—are not a part of your SG&A. By definition, these items are "other income" or "other expense" items. As a general rule, if something happens in your business that is not a part of your normal business operations, it belongs in "other income" or "other expense."

Now let's take a look at how these three dials—revenue, COGS, and SG&A—can be used to improve gross margin and business value.

Take the following example. Commercial construction is incredibly competitive, with many big companies bidding as low as possible to get each job. I worked with a firm headquartered in the northeastern United States that was earning about $25 million a year in revenue.

One day I was speaking with Gregg, the owner. "What are your gross margins?" I asked. "In other words, out of every dollar billed, what percentage of your revenue remains after you pay for the delivery of the product or service?"

"It's about 8 percent right now," he said.

That's really tight, a very small margin, and margins that small make profits challenging. Practically speaking, in commercial construction, gross margins should be in the range of 12 to 15 percent.

"My real problem is the competition," he said. "In our area there's a tremendous amount of competition for the jobs that I'm bidding on. To get them, I have to lower prices."

"I understand. Then what is your number one expense that goes into your cost of goods sold, that is, the finished jobs?"

"Well, I'm a general contractor, so I use subcontractors for most of the work—and paying subcontractors makes up most of the cost of each job."

"How are you doing on those costs now?"

"I try to bid the jobs at 10 percent to 12 percent gross margin, but sometimes we get a little slippage, so in practice I'm at about 8 percent gross margin."

I told him we needed to find a way to get his gross margin to 12 or 13 percent.

An improvement in his gross margin to 12 or 13 percent is a change of at least 4 percentage points to gross margin. That may not seem like a lot, and for most businesses it is pretty easy to either cut cost of goods sold by a couple percent or increase prices by a couple percent. In this case, raising prices was out of the question, so there was only one place to look to increase gross margins: cost of goods sold (more specifically, the amount he was paying his subcontractors).

This was going to be difficult, but it was worth the effort. On $25 million in revenue, without any increase in operational costs (SG&A), that 4 percentage point increase to gross profit margin meant $1 million more in annual net operating profit.

Prior to any change in gross profit margin, by the way, this construction company was making about $600,000 a year in profit on $25 million in revenue. With a simple 5 percent increase to gross profit margin, this company would realize a 300 percent increase in their net operating income. Needless to say, changes like that are worth the effort.

Revenue or sales	$25 million	$25 million
Gross profit/gross margin	2.4%	7.4%
Net operating income	$600,000	$1.85 million (+300%)

We started brainstorming. How could Gregg improve his gross profit and thus his gross margin? There are two things any business can do, and we discussed both options. He could increase revenue on the same cost base; however, this was not possible in his case. The competition was too tight, and the job pricing too competitive for him to raise his prices.

Alternatively, he could lower the costs of completing the job or finished product by trimming the costs of doing the work or producing the product. Those costs are called "cost of goods sold," and they became the focus of our analysis.

"You said something interesting about your subs," I told him. "I'm familiar with the construction industry, and subs constantly need cash."

"Yeah, it's terrible," he said. "That's what I worry about. I worry about bidding out work to a sub that doesn't have enough cash to finish the job. That's why I have more cash on hand than I need to run the business. I may have to bail one of them out or step in and take over if they run out of money."

"Let me ask this: If you gave your subs cash up front for the jobs or said you would pay them within thirty days after a job, and didn't require the 10 percent retention that most construction jobs have, how would they react? Would they lower their prices to you? Do you think you could get a 3 or 4 percent discount?"

"I'm certain I could get a 10 percent discount."

"Let's test that theory on one of your current jobs. I think you can use that cash to increase your gross margin."

"I'm willing to give it a try, but I want to be careful. Let's still pay them after the job is done, so that we don't end up paying them and having them leave. But let's pay them quickly, and let's agree that we will put the money aside to pay them so they know it's there. If they will give me a discount, I'll pay them as soon as the job is done, and I'll put the money in an escrow account so they know they'll get paid.

I'll just ask for 5 percent—I don't want them to cut into their profit so much that they go out of business."

"Now," I said, "look what that does to your cost of goods sold. By decreasing your cost of goods sold by 5 percent, your gross profit margin percentage is going to improve from 8 percent to 13 percent. You'll make $1 million more in profit."

"Matt, I'm still worried about keeping cash on hand," Gregg said.

I made some introductions to bankers that I knew would appreciate his type of business. I explained that he could go to a bank and get a revolving line of credit. He needed roughly $1 million in cash for approximately 90 days in order to make this happen. The $1 million line of credit cost him $60,000 a year in interest and fees. The deal was easy to sell to the bankers and to the business owner. $60,000 in fees got the business a $1 million line of credit, which allowed the business to make an extra $1,250,000 in net operating profit.

Profits skyrocketed from $600,000 to $1,850,000, a 300 percent increase; meanwhile, twelve months after the transaction, the business had an additional $700,000 of cash in the bank. In six months, the business would no longer need the line of credit. Perhaps most importantly, the value of Gregg's small general contracting business jumped from about $3 million to $9.25 million. This was a gain to his family of $6 million, and the increase in business value meant that one day he could sell the business and retire or just hire a general manager and spend more time with his family.

The lesson here is that even a slight increase in the gross margin, whether effected by increasing revenue or by cutting expenses, has a massive impact on the bottom line. Take a close look at what your business is doing with pricing. Examine all of your cost of goods sold very carefully. Consider all vendor and supplier relationships and work hard for an extra 1–4 percent increase to your current gross profit margin percentage. In a business with 10 percent net profit margins, you can sell 30 percent more or simply improve gross margins by 3 percent. Either way, you increase your net operating income by 30 percent.

However, all of this analysis is worthless if your financial accounting numbers are incorrect. Further, to be able to do this, you need to know your company's business model and how it compares to the elements that comprise your net operating income—that is, your revenue, COGS, and SG&A.

Fine Tuning the Dials

Let's return to our doughnut business and put some figures to these dials to see how they work. Start with revenue of $100 and COGS of $60. Revenue minus COGS equals gross profit. So our gross profit, or margin, is $40. We sold $100 worth of doughnuts (and delivery), it cost us $60 to make and provide, and we have $40 left over to pay for other expenses.

Next in the equation, we have SG&A. Our doughnut business has a storefront, office, marketing materials, price sheets, accounting expense, etc. In this business, let's say we have $30 of SG&A. Subtract $30 from $40 and we have $10 left over. That's our net operating income, or NOI.

Revenue or sales	$100
COGS	($60)
Gross profit/gross margin	$40
SG&A	($30)
NOI	$10

Along comes a lawsuit. This is not part of the normal course of business. It is not, say, the cost of electricity. It is not the cost of salaries. Where do we put this number? It would appear on the income statement below the NOI on a line that says "Other Income and Expenses." These are either income or expense items that are not a part of your normal course of business. For a small business owner, there might be a fair amount of these "other" things. Remember, the purpose of this first bottom line, NOI, is to determine whether we are operating our business successfully.

Another expense that's classified as an "other expense" but is commonly misunderstood is interest cost. I talk to many business owners who say they cannot operate without a bank loan, and many times they are correct. However, that does not make the interest cost on their loan an operating expense.

Here is the proof: Suppose I gave you as much money as you needed for no interest at all. Would you need a bank loan anymore? Of course not. What if you had a rich uncle who gave you all the money you needed to operate your business? You wouldn't need the loan any longer, and you would be able to cut your interest expense entirely.

If you could find a source of interest-free financing for your business, interest charges would not be incurred, but your business would still operate. Owners need to pay interest charges if they want financing and to get the cash they need, but interest is not required to operate the business.

Now, let's look at how we can use this first bottom line of net operating income to figure out how to make more money. This is where you can see the beauty and power of the math.

Going back to our example of the doughnut business, we start with revenue of $100. Let's say we sold 20 percent more, and so instead we have revenue of $120. Our COGS remains constant at 60 percent of revenue, so it now rises to $72 because we are producing more. We need more flour and sugar for those doughnuts. The SG&A is not going to change, necessarily. It is still $30. And so, net operating income is now $120 minus $72 minus $30, which equals $18. We had to sell 20 percent more to raise that net operating income figure by just $8.

Revenue or sales	$120
COGS	($72)
Gross profit/gross margin	$48
SG&A	($30)
NOI	$18

Now, let's take a look at what happens if we increase prices by 5 percent. Revenue increases from $100 to $105. COGS is still only $60, because all we did was raise prices; we did not produce more. The SG&A stays the same at $30. Our profit is $105 minus $60 minus $30, which equals $15. We gained $5 of net operating income without any increase in sales. It took only a slight increase in prices, and the result was nearly as good as all the effort to increase production by 20 percent.

Revenue or sales	$105
COGS	($60)
Gross profit/gross margin	$45
SG&A	($30)
NOI	$15

Let's try something even better. Say we don't change sales, but we do decrease COGS by $6, or 10 percent. We start out with $100 in revenue, but then our COGS is only $54. The SG&A remains at $30. The net operating income is $16 ($100 minus $54 minus $30). How would we go about decreasing the COGS to get that kind of result? There are many ways: discounts for early pay, discounts for larger bulk orders, discounts for long-term contracts, discounts by using a bid process, providing a deposit, increasing the order to include multiple products from the same vendor, etc.

Revenue or sales	$100
COGS	($54)
Gross profit/gross margin	$46
SG&A	($30)
NOI	$16

What do we learn from these examples? In short, often the best choice is to raise prices or control costs rather than to increase production. If we cut our costs by a dollar, whether in the SG&A or in the COGS, how much more do we have in net operating income? We have one more dollar of profit. However, if we add $1.00 in sales, our bottom line only improves by $0.40. If the shop sells one more doughnut for $1.00, we make $0.40.

Raising prices is far more efficient for the bottom line than selling more—but it is hard to tell that to CEOs and entrepreneurs, who by their nature are driven to sell. Entrepreneurs are constantly thinking about how to sell more, grow the business, and expand. Raising prices most likely will not help grow individual sales. Often this is the fallacy of playing offense. Sales is offense. Grow. Expand. Build. But unprofitable growth may not help you achieve your personal goals.

As illustrated in the earlier example, if you can increase prices by just 2 percent and cut supply costs by 2 percent, you will have a combined increase in gross margin of 4 percent—and (drum roll) you will see a 40 percent increase in net income.

What is the ripple effect of this type of excellent financial management? Number one, we are making more money. Also, most business owners at some point in life want to sell their business or at least maximize the value of their business. Since most businesses are valued on a multiple of earnings, the implications of a 40 percent increase in net income are huge—a 40 percent increase in net income equals a 40 percent increase in the value of the business.

If the business was worth $1 million before making a 4 percent change in gross margin—2 percent higher prices, and 2 percent lower supply costs—it is now worth $1.4 million. The value of the business has increased substantially with relatively small adjustments to pricing and supply costs. The valuation increases also have implications for loans and financing options for the business.

Revenue or sales	$100	$102
COGS	($60)	($58)
Gross profit/gross margin	$40	$44
SG&A	($30)	($30)
NOI	$10	$14
Value of business	$1,000,000	$1,400,000

$1 MILLION $1.4 MILLION

2% Higher Prices   2% Lower Costs

Heads You Win, Tails You Win

Gross margin is the most powerful accounting and financial metric for small business.

Imagine that one of your major customers came to you and said, "We like working with you, but if you don't want me to take this out to bid, I need you to give me just a 2 percent discount on the cost. Can you do that for me?"

This is a good customer, and you don't want to lose the revenue. Additionally, your competitiveness kicks in and you want to win the business. Then you remember the positive benefits of increasing gross margin, and you wisely decide to use the numbers to help you make this decision.

Let's run through the math to see how a 2 percent discount affects the business. Assume you have $100 in revenue before the discount. If you give a 2 percent discount, you are now at $98 in revenue. Subtract from that the COGS, which is still at $60 because you did not produce less. Nor have you changed the SG&A of $30. Therefore, your net operating income, which had been $10 before the discount, is now $8 ($98 minus $60 minus $30), or $2 less.

Revenue or sales	$98
COGS	($60)
Gross profit/gross margin	$38
SG&A	($30)
NOI	$8

By giving that customer a 2 percent discount, you have lost $2, which is 20 percent of your net operating income. And what did you do to the value of your business? You lost 20 percent of that, too. If it was worth $1 million before the discounting, it is worth

$800,000 afterward. In essence, you lost $200,000 by giving a 2 percent discount on your price.

Once you see the full impact of discounting on a business and its value, you will see how you might not want to make a quick decision on discounting.

Now, let's turn the power of the mathematics to your advantage. Let's look at it a different way. When that major customer asks for a discount, suppose you offered this: "I'll tell you what: I can't give you a 2 percent discount, but what I can do is let you pay me in 180 days instead of in 30 days. And if you want to do it that way, I will charge you just 1 percent more for the financing fee."

That's the other side of the coin. People either want a discount, or they want better terms of payment. Assuming that you collect on the deal, look at what you have accomplished by gaining that 1 percent: your revenue of $100 has increased to $101. Your COGS and SG&A haven't changed, so your net operating income has increased to $11 ($101 minus $60 minus $30). You increased NOI by 10 percent. You negotiated a mutually beneficial arrangement for yourself and your best customer, and you also improved your business valuation by 10 percent.

Revenue or sales	$101
COGS	($60)
Gross profit/gross margin	$41
SG&A	($30)
NOI	$11

Here's another possibility: Suppose you could get a discount from your suppliers by paying them earlier? Most people would recommend that you hold on to your cash; it would make no sense to pay earlier than necessary. But if you can get a discount, it makes a lot of sense. You're getting a discount that improves gross margin, and it will improve not only your net operating income but also the valuation of your business—and that can be worth many thousands, perhaps millions, of dollars.

CHAPTER 7

Cash from Operations and Net Equity

In this chapter, we will examine the other two parts of the Triple Bottom Line—cash from operations and net equity. Net cash from operations indicates how well you are managing cash flow. Net equity tells you whether your business is on secure financial ground—is your business getting stronger, or is it getting weaker?

Cash from Operations

Cash from operations tells you where your cash went. Your income statement, remember, does not tell you where your cash went. Think of Bill, from chapter 4, who got four months' credit on his rent in return for a long-term lease. In accrual accounting, those "free" months still show up on the income statement as cash paid out. The total is prorated to include those months. That provides a clear picture as to whether Bill's chocolate business made money in those months.

But Bill still wants to understand where his cash went, and he wants to make sure he does not run out of cash. That's what the bottom line of net cash from operations will show him.

It is a relatively straightforward measurement. For a small business, I recommend using what is known as the "indirect method" of preparing a cash flow statement. Using this approach, you are constantly looking to figure out what cash you are getting out of your operating business. This works for most businesses.

Remember, Bill's operating business is what is reflected in his income statement. He may ask, "How well did I sell and fulfill, and how much money is left after that?" Income is always the starting point in a net cash from operations calculation. Bill should start with how much revenue he earned and then ask how much of it he collected. How much did he earn that he did not receive? Let's say he starts with no cash, but he has revenue of $100,000 for a month. That's good, but he collected only $80,000 of that. His accounts receivable would go up by $20,000 because he did not collect the full $100,000 of revenue. This is where many business owners get hung up; it is a little counterintuitive. The change in accounts receivable means that Bill did not collect some money, and if he did not collect it, it means cash is less by the amount he didn't collect.

So in computing net cash, Bill starts with $100,000 earned and then subtracts the $20,000 that he did not collect. After that, he looks at money he spent on things that he has not yet received. Perhaps he bought $10,000 in office furniture and had to pay a 50 percent deposit up front. He hasn't received the furniture yet, so he hasn't expensed the $5,000 deposit. It therefore didn't affect his net income figure—but it does show up as a negative to cash. So he subtracts the $5,000 deposit from the cash account.

Here's what's happening with Bill's cash, then: He started the month at $100,000. His accounts receivable went up $20,000, which was the amount he didn't collect. That leaves him with $80,000 in cash. Then he paid $5,000 in advance for the furniture he will be getting. That leaves him with $75,000 in cash at the end of the month.

When you break it down, there are a couple more technical wrinkles in a statement of cash flow, but this is all that CEOs or business owners really need to worry about. The most important thing to know is whether the net cash from operations is positive. If it is positive, that means you are bringing in more cash for the month than the cash you're paying out. Your operational activities generated dollars.

Remember that net cash from operations does not tell you whether you were profitable; you learn that from the net operating income. Net cash from operations just tells you whether you brought in cash in excess of your cash expenses.

Cash is king, because if you run out of it you are out of business. However, a myopic focus on cash leads to unprofitable decisions that ultimately cause businesses to run out of cash.

Take the following example: Denny was running his commercial furniture business. Things appeared to be going well. Sales were up, and he was considering expanding and adding another location. To expand, Denny needed cash for a down payment on the new building. So, he went to one of his customers and asked if they would prepay for their next order if he gave them a 5 percent discount. They obliged. Denny got his cash, put it down on the new building, and was off and running. However, there was a problem. He still had to fulfill the order, and unfortunately he did not have the cash to do it. He quickly went back to his old cash generation strategy. He went to numerous customers and gave 5 percent discounts for early payment. Without recognizing the full impact of his decisions, Denny had just cut his profit margins from 8 percent to 3 percent. With all the expenses of the new store, the total profitability of his two stores went from 8 percent to negative 4 percent. He had lost profitability. Now, without profits, he could not get a loan from the bank. Without profitability, he had no hope of future cash coming in. Within six months, the healthy 8 percent profit business had turned negative. Denny had borrowed from customers and gave up his profitability.

The moral of the story is that cash is king, but profits generate cash. There is always a funding (cash) strategy for profitable businesses. Nobody wants to give cash to a money-losing operation. Therefore, if cash is king, then profits are the food that sustains it.

Net Equity

Net equity in your business is like the equity in your house—a concept that most people understand and appreciate. The more equity you have in your home and the lower your mortgage, the less likely you are to lose your house if you have a hiccup in cash resources.

It works that way with a business, too. If Bill owes less money and has more equity in his business, he stands a better chance of keeping it if his business hits a snag or the economy in general slows. In other words, his net equity is a measure of financial strength. His aim should be to constantly improve his financial strength, his solid position, his safety, his security. When he does, he has a lower chance of failure.

Net equity is what you own minus what you owe. If your house is worth $500,000 and you owe $200,000 on it, your net equity is $300,000. If Bill's business has assets of $1 million and he has liabilities of $400,000, he has net equity of $600,000.

As you look at your Triple Bottom Line, you want to make sure that your net equity is going up every month. It is as simple as that. If, as the CEO, Bill is constantly trying to figure retained earnings and sort out whether he has equity reconciled, or whether the deferred revenue is adequate, then he is looking at the wrong things. His accounting department should be taking care of that. For Bill, the most important thing is to look at the bottom line for net equity and make sure it is going up. If it is, the company is getting stronger.

If that figure is falling, he has to figure out why the business is getting weaker. What is he doing that's causing the problem? When a business is strong, opportunities open to make it even stronger. For example, most businesses have loans. Why do they have loans? Because loans are generally better for a business than using its own cash. But a business can't get a loan until it gets to a position of strength. Bankers do not give money to people who will not pay it back.

Net equity, in other words, is a metric that shows how capable a business is of withstanding problems. We saw so many home foreclosures as a result of the 2007–2008 recession because people were overleveraged—they owed too much compared to the value of what they owned.

As a business owner, you must not let that happen. You must be vigilant. If the equity in your business is going down, you need to investigate immediately.

CHAPTER 8

Key Performance Indicators

A diligent businessperson will want to keep on top of how the business is performing and will be looking for various ways to measure and to evaluate the success of the enterprise overall and its specific activities. These metrics are known as key performance indicators or KPIs.

What is the benefit of KPIs for your business? KPIs are diagnostic tools that give you a more in-depth understanding of your business's health and fitness than the Triple Bottom Line. The Triple Bottom Line provides a first level of information about the fundamental health of your business based on the periodic financial statements. Is it alive, on life support, or generally in good health? KPIs give you a more granular perspective on the business's daily operations. It's the difference between your doctor taking your blood pressure, which will give an indication of general health, and having tests run on a blood sample, which will show specific characteristics about the composition of your blood and enable your doctor to develop an accurate diagnosis of any adverse conditions indicated by the blood tests.

For a business, KPIs provide tools to analyze specific aspects of the business's operational health without spending a lot of time or effort. Not only are KPIs a time saver, but accurate metrics lead to better decisions, and that means more money. And there's an ancillary benefit of accountability: If everyone in the firm knows about the KPIs that you are using, they will tend to perform at or above those levels. If their performance falls below those levels, you will have a clear path for rectifying that situation.

The individual KPIs will tell you how particular operational pieces of your business are doing—and from that you can extrapolate what you need to do to improve. You might think of a KPI as a litmus test, or as the canary in the mine shaft. It gives you advance notice when there is trouble brewing.

Here I will focus on three KPIs, each related to one of the elements of the Triple Bottom Line. They are contribution margin, current ratio, and days sales outstanding.

Contribution Margin

Net operating income is one of the elements of the Triple Bottom Line. The contribution margin KPI lets you determine the effect on profitability of individual operating expenses that you incur in conducting your business. By making more expenditures that have a higher contribution margin and reducing or eliminating those that have a lower contribution margin, you can increase your business's overall net operating profit.

In previous chapters, we defined gross profit and gross margin. Gross profit is simply your revenue minus your cost of goods sold (COGS). To get your gross margin, you divide that result by your revenue, which gives you the percentage.

That's not the same as contribution margin, but it is very close. Contribution margin is your gross margin percentage minus any "variable costs" that you might have expressed as a percentage of revenue. Variable costs are those that fluctuate with the amount of revenue you have, such as sales commissions.

Here are a few examples of variable costs:

- Materials—The cost of your raw materials is usually directly related to the quantity of products produced.

- Royalties—Royalties are usually directly related to sales revenue.

- Direct labor—Hourly and other direct labor usually fluctuates with the amount of work being done. The amount of work being done is directly related to the amount of goods and services being produced.

- Any other cost that goes up every time a business sells something.

To determine the contribution margin for our doughnut business from chapter 6, we need to know our gross margin. To determine gross margin, we need to know how much of what we make in a sale must be spent to produce our goods or service, that is, our COGS. If we have $100 in revenue and $40 in COGS, we have $60 in gross profit. Expressed as a percentage, the $60 gross profit equals a gross margin of 60 percent of the $100 revenue.

To compute our contribution margin, we need to start with our gross margin and then subtract our variable costs, expressed as a percentage of revenue. Let's assume that we pay 10 percent sales commissions. We have a 60 percent gross margin from which we subtract the 10 percent sales commission figure, which gives us a 50 percent contribution margin.

	60% Gross Margin
-	10% Sales Commission
	50% Contribution Margin

Why is contribution margin important? Primarily because it gives us the basis for preparing a break-even analysis for our business. Using the contribution margin, we can tell exactly how much we need to sell in order to break even. That will give us peace of mind because we know that we will not lose money if we sell at least the amount needed to break even. And once we know the break-even number, we can assess whether hitting that number is realistic, and we can also be assured that if we sell more it's all profit.

In the example, we have $100 in revenue and $40 in COGS, which gives us a 60 percent gross margin. We subtract our selling commissions of 10 percent, and that gives us a 50 percent contribution margin. The question, then, is how much do we need to sell, at a 50 percent contribution margin, to break even on a monthly basis?

Revenue or sales	$100
COGS	($40)
Gross profit/gross margin	60%
SG&A	(10%)
NOI	50%

First, we look at our fixed expenses. These are expenses that we have to pay, which typically are our general and administrative expenses: the rent, the utilities, the administrative payroll, etc. Let's say our business has $50,000 a month in fixed expenses. How much would we need to sell to break even?

To get the answer, we divide the fixed costs by the contribution margin. That is, we divide $50,000 by 50 percent. The result is $100,000. We need to sell that much. That example makes it seem simple, but it's harder to see when the contribution margin is, say, 37 percent. The formula always works, however. Again: The fixed costs divided by the contribution margin equals the break-even sales.

The break-even point is critically important. A business owner must first observe the principle of "I don't want to fail" before "I want to grow and do great things." If the business fails, the owner won't get the chance to do those great things. Keep in mind the priority of the three laws of business: (1) don't fail, (2) be profitable, and (3) hit your goals.

The second reason you want to know the contribution margin is that you can then start to create measuring sticks for things that otherwise might be vague and seemingly immeasurable, such as marketing costs. You can start to use the contribution margin to manage your marketing department to a fixed performance ratio—a real performance that has a real number attached to it.

I have often heard business owners tell me about their marketing department. The conversation often goes like this:

"So how is your marketing department doing?" I ask.

"I don't know," the business owner says.

"What do you mean?"

"The last time I talked to them, our Twitter followers were up 320 percent."

"What did that do for sales?"

"Nothing."

"Okay, well, what else did they do?"

"Well, our website traffic, our new unique visitors, is up 340 percent."

"And what did that do for sales?"

"Nothing. But we do have this beautiful new ad in the *Wall Street Journal*, by the way, and it's awesome."

"Great, and what did that do to sales?"

"I don't know."

Marketing is often a nebulous endeavor. No one thing drives the direct return on investment. If a business acquires a million-dollar piece of machinery, the owner can calculate the rate of return on that investment. How can you figure the rate of return on your marketing investment? You use the contribution margin. The contribution margin divided by the fixed marketing and sales cost will result in your marketing return on investment.

Most businesses start off with a marketing budget and then try to figure out what their sales should be, but they could also do it in reverse. If they start off with a sales number, they can figure out what their marketing budget should be. They can do it up the chain or down the chain.

For example, if we decide to start at the top, with sales, we could say, "We are going to do $1 million in sales over the course of the year, and we are going to have a contribution margin of 50 percent." Therefore, we are going to have $500,000 of contribution margin. Our return on investment needs to be from 7:1 to 10:1, so we are going to divide that $500,000 by a number from 7 to 10. That gives us from about $70,000 to $50,000 (depending on our requirements for ROI) in an annual marketing budget to deliver those sales.

As long as we track that ROI of 7:1 to 10:1, we will see how well the marketing efforts are actually performing. As you can imagine, salespeople want to sell. They care far more about selling than they do about price. We don't want salespeople who will sell at any price, and we don't want marketers who get customers for us at any cost. We want customers to come in at a reasonable cost, and we want sales that reflect the type of customers we want, who will pay the right amount, so we can make money. Ultimately, that's what all of this is for. If we track our marketing ROI between 7:1 and 10:1, we can ensure that the sales coming in will be those that are profitable for us.

If we want to go the other way, from the bottom up, we can take a marketing budget of, say, $50,000. Then we say, "We need our marketing ROI to be 8:1." That means we should have a contribution margin of $400,000, which is equal to our marketing expense multiplied by our ROI of 8:1. At that point we can realistically assess whether our business will produce that amount of contribution margin. Assuming it will, we divide $400,000 (the amount of contribution margin that we need from spending $50,000 on marketing to achieve an ROI of 8:1) by 50 percent (the percentage of our actual contribution margin), and the result tells us that by spending $50,000 for marketing we need to generate at least $800,000 in sales to achieve our ROI of 8:1 on marketing expense.

The key is that with the contribution margin analysis we have a way to track the performance of our marketing and salespeople. We're not just asking, "Did we sell?" We can find out how much we spent to sell and whether it actually delivered profitable sales that brought money to the bottom line.

Current Ratio

The current ratio is related to the net equity element of the Triple Bottom Line. Just as the net equity figure indicates the level of protection we have from failing as of a particular time, the current ratio indicates whether our business is likely to fail in its future operations in the short term. The current ratio is perhaps the single most important KPI. All businesses must track it. A current ratio, defined as current assets divided by current liabilities, will tell us whether our business is going to run out of money. If your current liabilities exceed your current assets, you are headed toward business failure. If, however, current assets exceed current liabilities, you have a margin of safety within which to continue your operations and don't have to cut expenses or put more cash into the business.

Current assets are either cash or assets that are going to be turned into cash in a very short time. What is a short time? It depends on the business cycle, but generally it's anything less than twelve months.

For example, accounts receivable would be a current asset. If we have customers who have not paid when the sale was made, but we know they are going to pay and have recorded their debt to the business as a receivable, then that receivable is a current asset. Inventory would be another. It's a current asset if we expect to sell it in the next twelve months. And another current asset (one so obvious that a lot of people miss it) is cash in the bank.

Those are the typical current assets for most businesses. We would not list such things as property, machinery, plants, and equipment. Special attention should be given to shareholder loans that are unlikely to be paid back within twelve months.

What are current liabilities? Current liabilities include money that is going to be sucked out of a business sometime within the next twelve months. Debt is one, but only the portion of that debt that the business will be paying over the next year. Anything greater than that is considered a long-term liability. That's an important point to understand.

Other examples of current liabilities include payroll, vacation accruals, and PTO accruals. Also included are items from accounts payable, which includes purchases for which the business owner has yet to send the money. Those are all short-term liabilities.

In short, current assets include either cash or things that will soon become cash. Current liabilities include the things that soon will pull the cash out. Clearly, you want more of the former and fewer of the latter.

CURRENT ASSETS = CURRENT LIABILITIES

A 1:1 ratio of current assets to
current liabilities means you have zero cash.
A business should have anywhere from 1.5:1 to 4:1
ratio of current assets to current liabilities to stay afloat.

What happens if the amount of cash that you are going to have is equal to the amount of cash that's going to get sucked out? That would be a ratio of 1. How much cash will remain? Zero. If the current ratio slips to less than 1, that means you are flat-out going to run out of cash. Unless you can increase your sales at a faster rate than you are increasing expenses or you can cut expenses without sacrificing sales, you are in deep trouble.

$$\frac{\text{Current Assets}}{\text{Current Liabilities}} = \frac{1}{1} = \textbf{0 CASH}$$

$$\frac{\text{Current Assets}}{\text{Current Liabilities}} = \frac{1.5}{1}$$

The good news about the current ratio is that you can use it like the canary in the coal mine. If it tells you that you are running out of cash, that doesn't necessarily mean it will happen tomorrow. It means you are going to run out of cash in a short period. It's an indicator that gives you the ability to go do something about it.

To make more money, you have only the same three options as anyone else: You can sell more, you can cut costs, or you can get some financing or investment. That's it. Those are the only three things you can do; and if your current ratio is less than 1, you'd better be doing one of those right now. If you don't, you will run yourself out of business.

It is important that these assets and liabilities be classified correctly, which often does not happen. Often, businesses do not include their lines of credit, which are renewed and have to be paid off every year, in current liabilities. That's a major problem. Often, they do not have inventory in their current assets. That's another problem.

A current ratio is a measure of safety. More to the point, it is a measure of a business's ability to pay its bills in the next three to twelve months. Because the current ratio represents cash coming in divided by cash going out, a current ratio less than one means that a business is going to run out of cash. A strong current ratio indicates solid, conservative fiscal management.

Conservative fiscal management has benefits that extend well beyond the day-to-day operations of the business. For example, banks look very favorably at a strong current ratio. Banks will generally not lend to companies with current ratios lower than 1.5 and will very generously loan to companies with current ratios above 3. Bankers do not care how fast you are growing. Bankers do not care if you have an excellent product. Bankers do not care if you are an amazing salesperson. Bankers do not care about your people, and they really don't care about the "relationship." All of those things sound good in an initial meeting, but the bottom line is this: Bankers want to get repaid…that's it. Bankers look for conservative companies that are likely to repay them.

Additionally, investors (potential buyers) for your business are looking to invest in companies to get a return on capital. More important, look to Warren Buffett's two rules of investing:

1. Don't lose money.

2. Refer to rule number one.

There are countless investing opportunities for investors. A strong current ratio indicates minimal risk. Minimal risk means a low chance of losing money, and a low chance of losing money is an investment worth making. If a company has a strong current ratio, it will receive a premium price from investors.

Days Sales Outstanding

In the last chapter, we saw how Gregg's construction firm used its balance sheet as a way to make more money. Through some adjustments in operations, it was able to increase its net operating income. By making more money, a company can also increase its net equity—its financial strength. In doing so, it opens opportunities to make yet more money—and increase the value of the business.

A business with conservative financial management will get a much better business valuation, because its perceived risk level will be lower than its competitors'. It will get lower loan rates, and it will experience fewer headaches in negotiating with suppliers, insurers, bonding companies, etc.

Remember that net equity is a measurement of what you own minus what you owe. For a lot of businesses, one of the things that they own is accounts receivable. It is the amount of money owed to the business by people to whom the business has either sold a product or provided a service. Generally, business owners want to collect accounts receivable pretty quickly, because the faster they collect them the more cash they have on hand. I have found that many business owners do not pay enough attention to how fast they collect money. It surprises me how few people understand the importance and power of this practice.

Days sales outstanding, or DSO, relates to cash flow, a component of the Triple Bottom Line. It measures how quickly you're turning sales into cash. With this calculation, you can estimate your average receivables collection period. In effect, this financial ratio shows you whether you are adequately managing your accounts receivable. It tells you exactly how long it is taking for your customers to pay you. That's it. The benefit of this indicator is that it shows you the opportunity to collect more of your cash. When you do, you need to borrow less and pay less interest. It is really that simple.

DSO also tells you, if you start watching the trends, whether you are selling the right product, whether you are selling it at the right price, whether you are selling to the right customers, and whether you have the right type of contracts in place. These are critical issues that affect the long-term health of your business. In the short run, though, if you can just collect more, and do it faster, then you do not need to use as much of your loans. That's a huge plus.

To understand DSO, assume that Gregg's construction firm has $1 million in accounts receivable and generally collects it over a sixty-day period. If he could collect that in thirty days, or twice as fast, how much additional cash would he have in his bank account? He would have $500,000 more. Now let's say that, like most business owners, he is paying interest on loans. If he has a $500,000 loan on which he pays 6 percent, he could save $30,000 a year in interest just by collecting thirty days faster.

Here's another simple example: Let's say Gregg's firm has an accounts receivable balance of $500,000. He has revenue for the period of $500,000. If he divides the former by the latter, he gets 1. Then he multiplies that by the number of days in the period—in this case, a thirty-day month. The result is a DSO of thirty. It takes him thirty days to collect.

Accounts Receivable: **$1,000,000**
$$\frac{\text{Accounts Receivable: } \$1{,}000{,}000}{\text{Revenue: } \$500{,}000} = 2 \times 60 \text{ days*} = \text{DSO of 120 days}$$

$$\frac{\text{Accounts Receivable: } \$1{,}000{,}000}{\text{Revenue: } \$500{,}000} = 2 \times 30 \text{ days*} = \text{DSO of 60 days}$$

*30 DAYS VERSUS 60 DAYS IS A 50% INCREASE IN CASH.

Let's change the example. Let's say that Gregg's accounts receivable is now $750,000 and his revenue is $500,000. What is the new DSO? He would divide $750,000 by $500,000 and the result would be 1.5; multiplying by thirty days gives him a DSO of forty-five. Look at the difference. Now he has $750,000 outstanding. Before, he had $500,000. How much less cash does he have in the bank? Remember the cash flow statement—receivables represent revenue earned but not collected. This was $500,000, but now it is up to $750,000. That's $250,000 Gregg has earned but has not collected. That's negative for cash, which means he has $250,000 less in cash than he should.

Other important uses for DSO include figuring out how you are running your business, whether your customer base is changing, whether or not the quality of the sales is changing (getting better or worse), and whether or not your contracts are effective. These are things that you can tell by watching DSO that you can't tell by just looking at whether you are making sales.

Let's say sales are going up, and Gregg's DSO is going up, too, but at a faster pace than sales. What that indicates is that the business is not getting quality sales—just more sales. That could be an even worse problem if the increased sales are to deadbeats, because there's nothing worse than working for free. The business may need better sales contracts. Business owners should not let their businesses be the path of least resistance for their customers or their banks. The DSO tells you how fast people are paying you and how good your customers are. It also shows how well you set expectations and fulfilled them. People are quicker to pay those they like and who are valuable to them. Otherwise, they tend to try to delay payment or not pay at all.

CHAPTER 9

The Happiness Metric

A startling statistic: More than three-quarters of business owners who were polled three years after they sold their company were unhappy with the sale for one reason or another.

Some of them just missed being active and involved. But for most of them, that was not the problem. They were on the move. They were off doing something new, not sitting on the couch watching *I Love Lucy* reruns. The reason they were unhappy, they reported, was that the sale price had missed their expectation.

Why had that happened? One reason is that they got into transactions with earn-outs and other provisions that reduced overall purchase price. Susan might have sold her T-shirt company for $10 million but only got $2 million up front, for example. The rest would come over the next several years if the company hit certain revenue targets and kept expenses under a certain level.

So Susan is dealing with all these "ifs," and often the "ifs" never come true. That sale price of $10 million turned out to be only $4 million, perhaps, and even that amount did not come for four years. Susan set up her transaction with high hopes, and then reality set in.

But even for those who end up getting the full price—the full $10 million, for example—was that enough? Did they end up feeling good about selling their business?

I have developed a formula that helps to test whether the money received is enough for financial freedom. Remember that more than three-quarters of a typical business owner's net worth is tied up in the business. Therefore, the transaction represents a massive liquidation event that gives the seller the freedom to do something else. I am careful not to call it "retirement," because a lot of folks never really want to retire. But I do call it "financial freedom," because ideally this should be a time when sellers can do what they want, when they want.

My formula produces a metric by which you can predict whether you have enough money. It works for anybody, not just for business owners. It is an equation that will help you answer the question "How much money will I need to be financially free and not have to work anymore?"

First, write down a figure that represents your monthly expenses: how much you would like to spend to live, to pay your bills, and to pursue your dreams. Let's say it is $15,000 per month.

Then, multiply that by twelve to get the annual figure—in this case, $180,000. That's how much income you anticipate wanting in a year so that you will feel content and satisfied.

Double that number, and add a zero at the end. So $180,000 times two equals $360,000, and when you add the zero, you get $3,600,000.

Now, add on the tax that you would need to pay. That will vary from state to state, but let's say it totals 25 percent. That comes to $4,500,000.

FINANCIAL FREEDOM

$15,000 Monthly Expenses

x   12 Months

$180,000 Annual Expenses

$3,600,000 Double the number and add a zero

x   .25 25% tax (will vary by state)

$4,500,000 **NET WORTH** Financial Freedom

That is how much you need in net worth—not liquid net worth, but in total net worth—to be financially free. Most businesses sell for between three and five times earnings, and at most seven times earnings.

Let's return to Susan, who is selling her business for $10 million. She has a proposal under which she is going to get $2 million up front, and then she is going to get $8 million, paid over the next four or five years. What if she could take a different deal and get $5 million up front and then only $3 million over the next four or five years?

That way, by getting the $5 million up front, she would guarantee that she would be financially safe and free—even if she never received that additional $3 million.

So the purchase price would drop from $10 million to $8 million, a reduction of $2 million. But Susan's needs would be met because she knows her number, and she knows what she needs to be financially free. Anything above that, of course, she would be fine with. She can set her expectation level, based on this number, and use it to help negotiate a transaction for her business that makes sense for her.

So that is where the happiness question comes in. It is not about the dollars. It is about whether those dollars are meeting your needs. Everybody's needs will be different. But you have to know what your number is so that you can make an educated decision on the sale price that will work for you.

If you are a typical business owner, you are going to go on to do something new. You are going to start something, or you are going to get involved in a nonprofit. You will stay active because that is your nature. And meanwhile, while you are doing that, you will have peace of mind. You will know that you are financially safe. That sense of security is critical to happiness.

The numbers provide that metric of confidence. By having accurate numbers, and knowing exactly what you will need, you can move forward without having any doubt about what life will be like after you are no longer running your business.

This is a starting point, a framework for calculating how well you need to do. If you have other dependable streams of income, then you will not need as much from the sale of your business. You would simply subtract that monthly income—whether it is Social Security or the proceeds from a portfolio—from your monthly expenses and use that figure to determine your target.

I developed this formula so that anyone can do the math easily on the back of an envelope or on a napkin. In the last hundred years, there was only one year when it would not have worked. That was in 1929. The formula stands. It has withstood the test of time.

Where Do We Go from Here?

As you may remember from chapter 3, Luca Pacioli, an Italian monk and mathematician of the fifteenth century, is known as the father of accounting. He founded the system of double-entry accounting still used today. In other words, the truth of accounting has not changed. It has been the same for more than five hundred years.

Double-entry accounting systems might seem complex. Why put down two things when only one thing has happened? But it is just a system for making sure that everything works. It is a way of double checking. A plumber turns on the water after soldering pipes together. If it leaks, something is not right. That's the way double-entry accounting works. It establishes that you have done things right.

It has proven the test of time. That alone should instill confidence in it. Double-entry accounting shows when you are getting the numbers right. Big businesses may have many complicated formulas and regulations, but for small businesses, 99.9 percent of their transactions have been done the same way for all of these centuries.

Few things in life are so black and white, but accounting is one of them. There is truly a right way and a wrong way. It is a truth worth repeating: The numbers are not the most important thing; they are the only thing. Accuracy with the numbers is mandatory. It just will not do to say, "It is close enough."

There's nothing revolutionary about what you have read in this book, nor is there anything particularly complex about it. The math is all addition and subtraction. It is nothing fancy. It is simple stuff that's all about doing the right thing all the time.

All of the calculations and formulas and indicators are age old. If you use them properly and accurately, you will do far more than fend off failure. You will soar to success. Fix the process, fix the people, make sure you get the numbers right—these are my fundamental beliefs about accounting.

People ask me all the time, "Matt, are you worried you are giving out your secret sauce?" Why would I be worried about it? It never struck me as something that I was giving away.

Warren Buffett made a comment at a recent investment conference that struck me as right on point. "We use value investing," he said, "and it's really the only type of investing there is." Buffett said he had no problem telling everyone how he invests and sharing the formulas he uses. After all, he said, few people will have the discipline to put them to practice.

I look at accounting the same way. The business owners who will meet their personal goals are the ones who have the discipline to make sure each transaction is correct, each financial statement is on time, no one is stealing from them, they are forecasting with all three financial statements, and they know where they are going.

They might not build a billion-dollar company. Some will be happy with a $45 million company that kicks off $1 million of income to them every year. Some will operate a small family business and run it well. Success comes in big and small packages. One way or another, they will succeed. Why? Because they have done the little things right.

It is my goal, through the TGG Way, to share those time-tested standards and best practices. In doing so, I am confident that I can make a difference. These are principles that can change the deplorable rate of small business failure. Faithfully followed, they will not only fend off failure but usher in booming growth. Our clients, using the Triple Bottom Line to gain a deeper understanding of what is happening in their business, have proven the power of the TGG Way. They have gained peace of mind and an ever-larger piece of the action.

The world of accounting has no new, grand formulas. You might even call it boring. What it does is this: It gives you the opportunity to succeed. It keeps you on track toward your goals. You can look to the future with confidence, knowing that everything is in its place.

TGG's Twenty Beliefs about Small Business Accounting

Following are twenty fundamental statements that I have come to believe about accounting. At TGG Accounting, we show this list to prospective clients. If they, too, can see the importance of these statements, then we know that we will be able to work together to take their business to the next level of success.

1. There is only one right way to do accounting: on an accrual basis.

2. Every penny matters.

3. Every transaction matters and must be categorized (no "miscellaneous expense" category).

4. Every transaction must have a matching source document.

5. Accounting processes and procedures should be 90 percent the same at every business.

6. Books must be closed each month, each quarter, and each year without prior period adjustments.

7. All balance sheet accounts must be reconciled at least quarterly (many accounts monthly).

8. Any items that go unreconciled and remain outstanding must be investigated and explained promptly.

9. Financial information should be presented using the inverted pyramid technique (big picture to minute detail).

10. To maximize visibility, the balance sheet and income statement must fit on one page (with detail in the notes).

11. Every business must have a cash flow forecast.

12. To understand the financial health of his or her business, every manager must look at the Triple Bottom Line.

13. Taxes must be reconciled to the books each year.

14. Each entity can use only one accounting file (regardless of how many lines of business it has), and each entity needs its own accounting file.

15. To provide the highest quality product, eliminate fraud, operate efficiently (at the lowest cost), and deliver continuity, an accounting department requires four team members.

16. Doing the right work at the right level reduces errors and maximizes efficiency.

17. Our value is accurate accounting matched with sound strategic planning and cash management advice backed up by the numbers.

18. Business and personal goals are a managerial accounting metric and must be present in every business discussion and decision.

19. All goals must be Specific, Measurable, Actionable, Realistic, and Timely (SMART).

20. We never compromise our ethics, break the law, or knowingly participate in any fraudulent activity.

Printed in the USA
CPSIA information can be obtained
at www.ICGtesting.com
JSHW012046200524
63494JS00017B/705

9 781599 325194